PENGUIN STUDENTS' GRAMMAR OF ENGLISH EXERCISES

Teacher's Edition (with Key)

Susan Firman & René Bosewitz

Penguin Books

PENGUIN BOOKS

Published by the Penguin Group
27 Wrights Lane, London W8 5TZ, England
Viking Penguin Inc., 40 West 23rd Street, New York, New York 10010, USA
Penguin Books Australia Ltd, Ringwood, Victoria, Australia
Penguin Books Canada Ltd, 2801 John Street, Markham, Ontario, Canada L3R 1B4
Penguin Books (NZ) Ltd, 182–190 Wairau Road, Auckland 10, New Zealand

Penguin Books Ltd, Registered Offices: Harmondsworth, Middlesex, England

First published 1988

Copyright © Susan Firman and René Bosewitz, 1988
All rights reserved

Set in Linotron 202 9/11 pt Plantin Medium

Reproduced, printed and bound in Great Britain by
Hazell Watson & Viney Limited
Member of BPCC plc
Aylesbury, Bucks, England

Designed by Jacky Wedgwood
Illustrated by Sean MacGarry

Except in the United States of America, this book is sold subject to the condition that it shall not, by way of trade or otherwise, be lent, resold, hired out, or otherwise circulated without the publisher's prior consent in any form of binding or cover other than that in which it is published and without a similar condition including this condition being imposed on the subsequent purchaser

CONTENTS

		page
1	Nouns	1
2	Articles	4
3	Pronouns	9
4	Question Words	17
5	Adjectives	21
6	Adverbs	26
7	Quantifiers	32
8	Modals	38
9	Tenses	48
10	Unreal Past	61
11	To + Infinitive/Infinitive without To	66
12	Gerund	73
13	Participles	79
14	The Passive	85
15	Question Tags	92
16	Conditionals	95
17	Indirect (Reported) Speech	104
18	Prepositions	113
19	Phrasal Verbs	122
20	Linking Words	127
21	Punctuation	135
	Answers to the Exercises	139

1 NOUNS

BIRD'S EYE BOX: Nouns

People who live in glass **houses** shouldn't throw **stones**. →	singular and regular/irregular plurals (Exercise 1)
Have you seen my **sunglasses** anywhere? →	compound nouns (Exercise 2)
He's making good **progress**. →	nouns generally used in the singular
Have you washed my **jeans**? →	nouns generally used in the plural (Exercise 3)
I'll see you at **Mary's** party. I think he's at a **directors'** meeting. →	possession: singular and plural (Exercise 4)

EXERCISE 1

Complete the following table with the correct noun (singular or plural). The first one has been done for you.

	SINGULAR	PLURAL		SINGULAR	PLURAL
1	glass	**glasses**	9		knives
2	secretary		10	key	
3		people	11	child	
4		shoes	12		boxes
5	fish		13	tomato	
6		ladies	14	photograph	
7	tooth		15		bushes
8	policeman		16		feet

EXERCISE 2

Combine a word from box A with a word from box B to form a compound noun. Then use the nouns to complete the sentences below, making the noun plural where necessary. The first one has been done for you.

A
ash   ear   arm   hand
head   house   news
note   rain   tooth

B
bag   book   brush   coat
chair   line   paper
ring   tray   work

1 Hadn't you better take your **raincoat**? It's awfully cloudy.

2 Have you seen today's _____? The Prime Minister's resigned!

3 I get the shopping on Thursdays and do all the _____ on Fridays, so the weekend's free for the family.

4 Could you pass me that _____? I want to have a cigarette.

5 What a pretty pair of _____! Are those diamonds?

6 Have you finished with the _____? I want to see what's on television tonight.

7 Now, you've got your razor and your shaving-cream, haven't you? What about your _____?

8 Why don't you sit in the _____? You'll be more comfortable.

9 If you pass me my _____, I'll give you the money now.

10 It's a good idea to write down new vocabulary in a _____. Then you can refer to it later.

EXERCISE 3

Complete the following by putting a circle round the correct word in the brackets.

Example: I must get my ((hair)/ hairs) cut.

1 Could you give me some (information/informations) about trains to Edinburgh?

2 Where have I put my (glass/glasses)? I can't read a thing!

3 Put it on the (scale/scales) so I can see how much it weighs.

4 I can't come out tonight. I've got a lot of (homework/homeworks) to do.

5 You'll find your clean (pyjama/pyjamas) in the cupboard.

6 They've got some lovely (furniture/furnitures), but just look at the price!

7 If you spoke to your solicitor about it, I'm sure he'd give you some (advice/advices).

8 Could you pass me the (scissor/scissors)? I can't cut this with a knife.

EXERCISE 4

Choose the correct word (a, b or c) to complete the sentence and write the appropriate letter in the box. The first one has been done for you.

1 You can't sit there. That's _____ place.
   (a) Alison   (b) Alison's   (c) Alisons'   **b**

2 Could you take these books to the _____ Room, please?
   (a) Teacher   (b) Teacher's   (c) Teachers'   ☐

3 We're going to a _____ party this afternoon.
   (a) children   (b) children's   (c) childrens'   ☐

4 Have you seen the _____ keys anywhere?
   (a) car   (b) car's   (c) cars'   ☐

5 That's Mrs Davies, the _____ wife.
   (a) doctor   (b) doctor's   (c) doctors'   ☐

6 I'm borrowing my _____ car while they're away.
   (a) parent   (b) parent's   (c) parents'   ☐

7 I must buy some new _____ curtains.
   (a) bedroom   (b) bedroom's   (c) bedrooms'   ☐

8 That's _____ bag, isn't it?
   (a) Terry   (b) Terry's   (c) Terrys'   ☐

2 ARTICLES

BIRD'S EYE BOX: Articles

	THE DEFINITE ARTICLE	
The girl who lives next door	→	a specified noun (Exercises 1, 2 and 7)
The earth travels round **the** sun.	→	a unique object (Exercises 1, 2 and 7)
The French, **the** rich	→	an adjective used as a noun (Exercises 1 and 7)
The best book I've ever read	→	superlatives (Exercises 1 and 7)
	ZERO ARTICLE	
Women live longer than men.	→	plural nouns in general statements (Exercises 1, 2 and 7)
Tom, Sweden, Friday, Easter, summer	→	names, countries, days, festivals, seasons (Exercises 1 and 7)
Time passes quickly.	→	abstract nouns (Exercises 1 and 2)
	THE INDEFINITE ARTICLE	
a man, **an** idea	→	singular nouns, not specified (Exercises 3 and 7)
Twice **a** day	→	expressions of frequency (Exercise 4)
£1.50 **a** metre	→	measurements (Exercises 5 and 7)
What **an** awful shock!	→	exclamations (Exercise 6)

EXERCISE 1

*Complete the following dialogues by putting **the** into the spaces only where necessary.*

1 'Excuse me. Can you tell me where (a) _____ nearest garage is?'
  'It's on (b) _____ main road, just after (c) _____ supermarket.'

2 'Who's that girl over there talking to (a) _____ man with red hair?'
'Oh, that's Sandra. She's one of (b) _____ girls I work with. She only started (c) _____ week before last.'

3 'Did you have a good holiday?'
'Yes, it was one of (a) _____ best we've ever had. (b) _____ hotel was comfortable, (c) _____ food was excellent and even (d) _____ beaches were clean. We're going back (e) _____ next summer.'

4 'Do you think (a) _____ men are better drivers than (b) _____ women?'
'Not necessarily. Some of (c) _____ worst drivers I know are (d) _____ men.'

5 'What's on at (a) _____ cinema? Anything interesting?'
'No. There's only a musical or a Western. We've seen (b) _____ Western before, and I don't like (c) _____ musicals very much.'

6 'Who put (a) _____ first man into (b) _____ space? (c) _____ America or (d) _____ Russia?'
'(e) _____ Russia. But (f) _____ Americans were first on (g) _____ moon.'

7 'Are you voting for (a) _____ Government in (b) _____ next election?'
'Certainly not. This Government has only made (c) _____ rich richer and (d) _____ poor poorer. And they've done nothing to help (e) _____ unemployed find (f) _____ jobs!'

8 'I don't agree that (a) _____ honesty is always (b) _____ best policy. Do you?'
'Definitely not. (c) _____ diplomacy is sometimes more important.'

EXERCISE 2

Complete the following speech by putting **the** *into the spaces only where necessary (not in every sentence).*

'We in (1) _____ West are very lucky. How often do we experience (2) _____ real poverty, (3) _____ oppression or (4) _____ natural disasters? (5) _____ life for us is fairly easy compared with (6) _____ life led by millions all over (7) _____ world. I have travelled far and wide and (8) _____ poverty I have seen in some countries is unimaginable. Every day (9) _____ people die from (10) _____ starvation and (11) _____ diseases caused by (12) _____ starvation. (13) _____ people in these countries need (14) _____ food and (15) _____ medicine urgently, and they are asking us for (16) _____ help. But we need (17) _____ money: your money. We cannot buy (18) _____ food they need, nor provide (19) _____ medicine they require without (20) _____ money you give today. So, please, give generously. Thank you.'

EXERCISE 3

*Put **a** or **an** before each of the following.*

1 _____ hotel
2 _____ hour
3 _____ unusual situation
4 _____ university education
5 _____ unidentified flying object
6 _____ horrible dream
7 _____ honest man
8 _____ union official

EXERCISE 4

A housewife talks about her family. Read what she says and then complete the exercise below. (You must work out how often each thing happens.) The first one has been done for you.

I take the dog for a walk every morning and evening and I go to keep-fit classes on Mondays, Wednesdays and Thursdays. So, as you can see, I get plenty of exercise! I've got two children. Tom, the elder, works abroad, but he comes home every three months or so. We always get at least a couple of letters from him every month. Sally, my daughter, has just got a boyfriend. He always phones her at eight o'clock in the evening and they talk for hours! We nearly always go away on holiday when school finishes, at Christmas, Easter and in the summer. Sometimes it's only for a few days and sometimes longer. I think we're basically a very close family.

1 She takes the dog for a walk **twice a day**.

2 She goes to keep-fit classes _____.

3 Tom comes home _____.

4 They get a letter from Tom at least _____.

5 Sally's boyfriend always phones her _____.

6 They go away on holiday _____.

EXERCISE 5

Using the information in the shopping list, complete the sentences below. The first one has been done for you. (Note: £1 = 100p)

5 kilos of potatoes	60p
2 loaves of bread	70p
½ dozen eggs	79p
3 pints of milk	69p
2 litres of orange juice	98p
4 cans of beer	£1.20
500 grams of butter	£1.11
1.5 litres of wine	£4.50

1. The potatoes were **12p a kilo**.
2. The bread was _____ a loaf.
3. The eggs were _____ a dozen.
4. The milk was _____.
5. The orange juice was _____.
6. The beer was _____.
7. The butter was _____.
8. The wine was _____.

EXERCISE 6

Complete the exclamations with a or an only where necessary (not in every sentence).

Examples: What **an** awful shock! What beautiful flowers!

1. What _____ lovely day!
2. What _____ nice people!
3. What _____ awful experience!
4. What _____ terrible noise!
5. What _____ dreadful weather!
6. What _____ well-behaved children!
7. What _____ good idea!
8. What _____ interesting story!
9. What _____ sad news!
10. What _____ idiotic thing to do!

EXERCISE 7

Complete the news items with the, a or an only where necessary.

Good evening. Here is (1) _____ nine o'clock news.

(2) _____ Prime Minister arrived in Washington this morning for (3) _____ talks with (4) _____ American President. (5) _____ talks are expected to start in (6) _____ morning.

(7) _____ Government has promised to give (8) _____ quarter of (9) _____ million pounds to help (10) _____ homeless in London. (11) _____ recent survey has shown that (12) _____ number of people without (13) _____ homes has doubled in (14) _____ last two years.

(15) _____ man was arrested in London this evening after (16) _____ 100 mile (17) _____ hour car chase along (18) _____ M4 motorway.
(19) _____ man has, so far, not been named.

(20) _____ lorry containing (21) _____ dangerous chemicals was stolen from outside (22) _____ factory in Epping over (23) _____ weekend.
(24) _____ spokesman for (25) _____ factory said (26) _____ chemicals were highly poisonous.

From midnight tonight (27) _____ petrol will cost (28) _____ extra 1p (29) _____ litre. (30) _____ rise is caused by (31) _____ present high price of (32) _____ oil in (33) _____ Middle East.

(34) _____ eighty-year-old man has become (35) _____ oldest person to cross (36) _____ Atlantic alone. Sam Taylor, from New York, arrived in Plymouth last night.

3 PRONOUNS

BIRD'S EYE BOX: Pronouns

I'll see **you** later.	→	personal pronouns (object) (Exercises 1 and 9)
Hey! That's **mine**!	→	possessive pronouns (Exercise 1)
I can't find **my** car keys.	→	possessive adjectives (Exercises 1 and 9)
She's staying with some friends **of hers**.	→	double possessive (Exercise 1)
These flowers are for you. **That's** mine!	→	demonstrative adjectives/ pronouns (Exercises 2 and 9)
He hurt **himself** quite badly.	→	reflexive pronouns (Exercises 3, 4 and 9)
They disliked **each other/one another** on sight.	→	reciprocal pronouns (Exercises 4 and 9)
Isn't he the man **whose** photo was in the paper?	→	relative pronouns (Exercises 5, 6, 7 and 9)
There's **no one** there.	→	indefinite pronouns (Exercises 8 and 9)
Didn't she say **anything else**?	→	indefinite pronouns + **else** (Exercises 8 and 9)

EXERCISE 1

David Garrick, Roger Warner and Bill Matthews have just interviewed several applicants for a job. Complete the following discussion by putting a circle round the correct pronoun or adjective in the brackets.

Example: The final decision is (me / my /(mine))

DAVID: Well, gentlemen, that's the last applicant, and now it's up to (1) (us/our/ours) to make a decision. It seems to (2) (me/my/mine) that there are only two possibilities: Jane Barratt and Michael Smith.

However, as (3) (them/their/theirs) qualifications are equally good and they've both got a lot of experience, it's difficult to choose between (4) (them/their/theirs). So, I'd like to hear (5) (you/your/yours) opinions first. Roger?

ROGER: Oh, I'd definitely give the job to (6) (she/her/hers). I liked (7) (she/her/hers) enthusiasm and felt (8) (she/her/hers) ideas were more up to date than (9) (he/his/him). To be honest, I was rather disappointed in (10) (he/his/him). I found (11) (he/his/him) rather dull. Well, that's (12) (me/my/mine) opinion. What's (13) (you/your/yours), Bill?

BILL: I don't really agree with (14) (you/your/yours), Roger. I got the impression she was rather neurotic. She reminded me of a friend of (15) (us/our/ours) who is very unreliable. I'd give (16) (he/his/him) the job and not (17) (she/her/hers). Don't forget, (18) (he/his/him) references are much better than (19) (she/her/hers).

ROGER: References! Who takes any notice of references! If I remember correctly, (20) (me/my/mine) weren't very good either, and I doubt if (21) (you/your/yours) were much better, Bill!

BILL: Speak for yourself, Roger! Anyway, it's no business of (22) (you/your/yours)!

DAVID: Gentlemen, if we could get back to discussing the candidates. Now, personally, I agree with . . .

EXERCISE 2

Complete the following with **this, that, these** *or* **those**. *The first one has been done for you.*

1 These are very pretty, aren't they? I particularly like <u>**this**</u> one. Don't you?

2 Who's that man talking to _____ people over there?

3 I like this bag, but it's rather expensive. How much is _____ one in the window?

4 This is my husband, Robert, and _____ are my children, Tom and Helen.

5 That knife's not very sharp. Here, use _____ one.

6 The postman's just been. This one's for me and all _____ are for you. Here you are.

7   These clothes over here are in the sale, madam, but _____ on the other side aren't.

8   Those children next door are dreadful, aren't they? And _____ boy Nigel is the worst!

EXERCISE 3

*Read the following pieces of conversation overheard at a party. Fill in the spaces with the correct reflexive pronoun (**myself, yourself,** etc.) only where necessary (not every time). The first one has been done for you.*

1   'Oh, it's nothing much really. I cut **myself** when I was opening a tin.'

2   'My eldest son's gone hitch-hiking in France. I suppose he can take care of _____, but I'm not very happy about it.'

3   'We had a few days' holiday in Morocco last month. We both thoroughly enjoyed _____ it.'

4   'Of course, we miss the boys now they've left home, but I must admit we do appreciate having more time to _____.'

5   'Thanks for coming to the party, Tony. I hope you're enjoying _____.'

6   'Well, I must say I thought she behaved _____ terribly badly under the circumstances.'

7   'Come on, everybody. There's plenty to eat and drink, so please help _____.'

8   'We've left the children with Jim's mother. I only hope they're behaving _____!'

EXERCISE 4

*Complete the following two letters with the correct reflexive pronoun (**myself, yourself,** etc.) or **each other/one another**.*

Examples: They haven't spoken to **each other/one another** since they quarrelled.
They should be ashamed of **themselves**.

Dear Rosemary,

You'll never guess who I heard from last week. Julie Saunders! We haven't seen (1) _____ for at least two years! Anyway, she's invited us to spend the weekend at her house in Sussex. I only hope Bill and Andrew get on with (2) _____ and that the children behave (3) _____!

I'll tell you all about it in my next letter. Meanwhile, take care of (4) _____.

With love,
Debbie

Dear Rosemary,

The weekend with Julie Saunders was quite successful. At least, Bill and I enjoyed (5) _____; Bill and Andrew liked (6) _____ immediately and spent most of the weekend discussing sport. Unfortunately, our children and Julie's two took an instant dislike to (7) _____! However, the weather was fine, so they were able to amuse (8) _____ in the garden, although they wouldn't play with (9) _____.

Of course, Julie and I had a lot to say to (10) _____, and the time just flew by. But we hope to meet (11) _____ in London one day. Why don't you come too? Anyway, in the meantime, look after (12) _____.

With love,
Debbie

EXERCISE 5

Complete the following newspaper article by choosing the correct pronoun from the box below. Use each pronoun twice only.

> who   whom   whose   which

Actress Buried in Hollywood

The actress Lilian Bell, (1) _____ died last week, was buried today in Hollywood. Miss Bell, (2) _____ career in films lasted more than forty years, was one of the great stars of the 1940s. Her most successful role was Catherine the Great in *The Russian Empress*, (3) _____ was directed by her first husband, Daniel Steinberg, from (4) _____ she was divorced in 1952. She later married the actor Peter Becker, with (5) _____ she made several films before his death in 1969. Hilary Marshall, (6) _____ biography of Miss Bell was published last year, said, 'She was a talented actress (7) _____ knew exactly what the public wanted. Her death is the end of an era (8) _____ produced some of the finest actors in the history of the cinema.'

EXERCISE 6

*You are showing holiday photos to a friend. Join the two sentences to make one sentence by using **who, which** or **whose** only where necessary. Sometimes other changes in the sentence will be required.*

Examples: That's the courier. She looked after us.
That's the courier who looked after us.

That's the beach. We went to it every day.
That's the beach we went to every day.

1 That's the Smith family. They had the room next to ours.
2 That's Señor Bueno. His daughter worked in the hotel.
3 That's the Tropicana Disco. We went to it a couple of times.
4 That's the local bookshop. It sold English newspapers.
5 That's the Pablo family. We met them on the beach.
6 That's Señora Pablo. Her brother works in London.

7 That's Roberto, the waiter. He showed us how to dance flamenco.
8 That's the hotel cat. It used to follow us to the beach.

EXERCISE 7

*Read the following news items and then join each of the pairs of sentences to make one sentence by using **who, which, whose** or **whom**. Sometimes there may be more than one acceptable answer.*

Example: Two youths have been fined £500 for starting a fire. They both have criminal records.
Two youths, who both have criminal records, have been fined £500 for starting a fire.

1 Heavy snow has blocked most roads in the north of Scotland. It fell unexpectedly during the night.
2 Cardinal Onzo of Brazil left from Heathrow this morning. The Archbishop of Canterbury had talks with him earlier this week.
3 Amateur radio enthusiast Paul Little saved the lives of nine Spanish seamen last night. He heard the SOS signal on his transmitter.
4 Simon Walsh, twenty-two, appeared at Manchester Crown Court today, charged with driving without a licence. His father is the Conservative M.P. for Lower Trauton.
5 A priceless seventeenth-century painting has been discovered in a house in Berkshire. It was stolen over twenty-five years ago.
6 Mr and Mrs Andrew Baker have received more than £200,000 compensation from their local council. Their house was demolished by mistake.
7 The famous 1920s beauty Nancy Loughborough has died in her sleep at eighty-two. The well-known song 'Beautiful' was written for her.
8 And finally, Mrs Brenda Tyler has been nominated Slimmer of the Year. She lost more than thirty-five kilos in six months.

EXERCISE 8

*Complete the following sentences with the correct pronoun (**someone/body, something**, etc.), using **else** where necessary.*

Example: I couldn't get any small tomatoes, but I got **everything else** on the list you gave me.

1 Do you think you could ask _____ to help you? I'm rather busy at the moment.
2 Has _____ seen my bag? I'm sure I left it on the table.

3   There's not much on television tonight. The film at nine o'clock might be OK, but there's _____ worth watching.

4   Derek's late again! Honestly, if _____ can get here on time, why can't he?

5   Do you want _____ to eat or drink, or shall I ask for the bill?

6   I've done _____ you asked me to do, Mr Elgood, so is it all right if I go home now?

7   Look, it's rather confidential. So, although I've told you, I don't want _____ to know. OK?

8   Come outside a minute, Jane. There's _____ I want to tell you.

9   Alice was there and so was Philip, but _____ came! So, as you can imagine, it was a pretty awful party!

10 Well, the police asked a lot of questions, but I couldn't help them, as I knew _____ about the people upstairs.

11 I've been to the bank, collected the dry-cleaning and paid the electricity bill. But I'm sure there was _____ I had to do.

12 _____ phoned you earlier, but he didn't leave his name.

EXERCISE 9

Complete the following speech by putting a circle round the correct pronoun or adjective in the brackets.

Ladies and gentlemen, could I have (1) (you/your/yours) attention for a moment? As you know, (2) (this/that/these/those) is a very sad occasion for all of (3) (us/our/ours), because we have to say goodbye to Duncan Saunders, (4) (who/whom/whose) retires today after twenty-five years with the company.

   Duncan has been here longer than (5) (someone else/anyone/anyone else), and we will miss (6) (he/his/him) very much. He has always been an enthusiastic worker, (7) (who/whom/whose) sense of humour cheered (8) (someone/anyone/everyone) up, especially on Monday mornings! He is a man I admire and respect enormously, even though, as he well knows, we haven't always seen eye-to-eye with (9) (ourselves/each other/us). And I'm sure he remembers (10) (this/that/these/those) arguments as well as I do!

Duncan, if you look at the contribution you have made to the company, you can be proud of (11) (you/yours/yourself). And to show (12) (us/our/ours) appreciation, we would like to give you (13) (anything/something/nothing else) to remember (14) (us/our/ours) by. And I am sure I'm not just speaking for (15) (me/each other/myself) but for (16) (anyone else/someone else/everyone else) too when I wish you and your wife a very happy retirement.

4 QUESTION WORDS

BIRD'S EYE BOX: Question words

What? Who? Where? When? Why? Which? Whose? How many/much/often/far/long? **What** did you do? **Where** did you go?	→	question words (Exercises 1, 2 and 5)
What else did you do?	→	question words + **else** (Exercise 3)
What time did you get home?	→	interrogative adjectives (Exercises 4 and 5)
What a good idea! **How** interesting!	→	exclamations (Exercise 6)

EXERCISE 1

Look at the answer in order to find the correct word or words to complete the question.

Example: '**Who** was that at the door?' 'Only the milkman.'

1 '_____ did you get back?' 'Saturday night.'
2 '_____ do you want to know?' 'I'm just interested, that's all.'
3 '_____ do you prefer?' 'I don't really like either of them.'
4 '_____ did you get home?' 'Peter gave me a lift.'
5 '_____ are these?' 'They're Graham's, I think.'
6 '_____ is it exactly?' 'On the outskirts of Birmingham.'
7 '_____ do you see him?' 'Only once or twice a year.'
8 '_____ was that?' 'I didn't hear anything.'
9 '_____ is it?' 'It's me.'
10 '_____ did you have to walk?' 'Only a couple of kilometres.'

EXERCISE 2

You are reading the following magazine article. Unfortunately, the page has been torn. Write down the questions you need to ask to find the missing information. The first one has been done for you.

> Another mystery is that of Lord Cluan, who disappeared in (1)
> The Cluan family, together with the children's nurse, lived in (2)
> Cluan was in serious financial trouble because of (3)
> which is probably the reason for the tragic events of that night.
> Cluan had gone out, but returned unexpectedly at about (4)
> The nurse, who was upstairs at the time, heard (5)
> and went downstairs to investigate. Cluan killed her by (6)
> It is now thought that he probably intended to murder (7)
> and not the nurse, but made a mistake because (8)
> After the murder, Cluan left and drove to (9)
> Police found his car the next morning. Inside the car they found (10)
> Cluan has never been seen since.

1 <u>When did Lord Cluan disappear?</u>
2 _____?
3 _____?
4 _____?
5 _____?
6 _____?
7 _____?
8 _____?
9 _____?
10 _____?

EXERCISE 3

*Complete the following with the correct question word + **else**.*

Example: I'm sure he's not telling us the whole truth. **Why else** would he look so guilty?

1 I said it was confidential. But Paula knows and Brian knows. _____ have you told?

2 Right. I've cleaned the bathroom, made the beds and tidied upstairs. _____ would you like me to do?

3 If it's not in your bag and it's not in your pockets, _____ could it be?

4 I'll just have to ask my father to lend me some money. _____ can I manage till the end of the month?

5 I think they must be in serious financial trouble. _____ would they consider selling the company?

6 I know you're free on Monday and Tuesday, but I'm a bit busy then. _____ could you come?

EXERCISE 4

Read the following job advertisement and write down the questions you would ask an applicant. The first one has been done for you.

EXPERIENCED (1) LANGUAGE TEACHER REQUIRED FOR SCHOOL IN OXFORD

University (2) education and good qualifications (3) essential. Must speak at least two languages (4). Preference will be given to applicants who have worked in countries (5) outside the United Kingdom. An interest in sports (6) is desirable but not essential.

1 **What experience** have you had?
2 _____ did you go to?
3 _____?
4 _____?
5 _____?
6 _____?

EXERCISE 5

Jenny is going to stay with Anne in Edinburgh. Read the following telephone conversation and write down the questions Jenny asks. The first one has been done for you. There may be more than one acceptable answer.

JENNY: (1) **Which station do the Edinburgh trains leave from?**

ANNE: King's Cross.

JENNY: (2) _____?

ANNE: I think there's only one train an hour.

JENNY: (3) _____?

ANNE: Every hour, on the hour. Nine o'clock, ten o'clock and so on.

JENNY: (4) _____?

ANNE: Well, I think the Flying Scotsman's the best train. It goes at ten o'clock.

JENNY: (5) _____?

ANNE: It takes about four and a half hours.

JENNY: (6) _____?

ANNE: I'm not sure exactly. I think a return's at least £60, but it's probably more.

JENNY: (7) _____?

ANNE: Meet me outside the station. I'll come and pick you up. I'm borrowing Peter's car for the day.

JENNY: (8) _____?

ANNE: Peter's.

JENNY: (9) _____?

ANNE: Peter? Oh, sorry. He's a friend of mine. You'll meet him while you're here.

JENNY: (10) _____?

ANNE: Oh, he's got a blue Maxi.

JENNY: (11) _____?

ANNE: Don't bring anything special. Just a pair of jeans and some walking shoes.

JENNY: (12) _____?

ANNE: Well, it depends on the weather, but I thought we might go to Loch Ness.

EXERCISE 6

Complete the following exclamations with **what** *or* **how** *and, where necessary, add* **a** *or* **an**.

Example: **What a** nuisance! **How** annoying!

1 _____ embarrassing!
2 _____ pity!
3 _____ bad luck!
4 _____ extraordinary!
5 _____ surprise!
6 _____ awful!
7 _____ exciting!
8 _____ lovely weather!
9 _____ rude!
10 _____ silly thing to say!

5 ADJECTIVES

BIRD'S EYE BOX: Adjectives

We need to protect **the young**.	→	adjectives used as nouns (Exercise 1)
The weather isn't very **nice**. It isn't a very **nice** day.	→	position of adjectives (Exercise 2)
She's **older** and **more experienced** than the others.	→	comparison of adjectives (Exercises 3, 4 and 6)
The latest model is also **the most expensive**.	→	superlative of adjectives (Exercises 3, 5 and 6)

EXERCISE 1

Complete the following extract from a history book by choosing from the box below. Do not use any word more than once. The first one has been done for you. Note that two words are needed in each space.

blind	good	homeless	old	poor	rich	sick	strong	unemployed
weak	wealthy	young						

Society, in those days, was divided into (1) **the rich** and (2) _____.
Life for (3) _____ was easy. They could send their children to school
and they could afford the best doctors. However, life for the vast majority was
very different. There was little education for (4) _____, no free
hospital treatment for (5) _____ and no state pensions for
(6) _____. (7) _____, who could not find jobs, were
frequently regarded as lazy, and (8) _____, who had nowhere else to
go, simply slept in the streets. It is not surprising, then, that only
(9) _____ survived. (10) _____ rarely lived more than a
few years.

EXERCISE 2

Change the order of the words to make a correct sentence.

Example: very/a/he's/man/difficult
> **He's a very difficult man.**

1 was/meal/delicious/that/really
2 difficult/the/look/exam/terribly/doesn't
3 a/embarrassing/very/it's/situation
4 seem/children/excited/the/very/didn't
5 programme/extremely/it's/interesting/an

EXERCISE 3

Complete the table with the correct forms.

	ADJECTIVE	COMPARATIVE	SUPERLATIVE
	young	younger	(the) youngest
1		more interesting	
2	far		
3		worse	
4	easy		
5			(the) most valuable
6	thin		
7			(the) eldest/oldest
8	aggressive		
9		wider	
10	good		

EXERCISE 4

Read the following reports on two hotels. Then compare them in the space below. There may be more than one acceptable answer.

The Supercontinental	The Glencairn Hotel
1 **Position**: 5 minutes from city centre	1 **Position**: 15 minutes from city centre
2 **Accommodation**: 80 rooms	2 **Accommodation**: 55 rooms
3 **Price**: £60–£85 per night	3 **Price**: £40–£55 per night
4 **Facilities**: restaurant, nightclub, pool, sauna	4 **Facilities**: restaurant, bar, tennis court
5 **Food**: wide choice on menu	5 **Food**: small choice but excellent
6 **Service**: efficient but impersonal	6 **Service**: a little slow but friendly
7 **Comments**: rather noisy	7 **Comments**: quiet and comfortable

The Supercontinental
1 **It's nearer the city centre.**
2 _____
3 _____
4 _____
5 _____
6 _____
7 _____

The Glencairn Hotel
1 _____
2 _____
3 _____
4 _____
5 _____
6 _____
7 _____

EXERCISE 5

Read the following notes from the diary of a mountaineer. Then complete the exercise below. The first one has been done for you.

Day 1 Didn't climb far. Fairly easy day.	*Day 4* Wind icy! Extremely cold!
Day 2 Climbed for eight hours. Very long day.	*Day 5* Weather appalling! A very bad day.
Day 3 Altitude made air thin. Very exhausting.	*Day 6* Impossible to climb. Very frustrating!

Day 7 Didn't make much progress. Extremely depressing.	Day 9 Reached the top at last! Tremendously exciting!
Day 8 Climb very difficult. A very hard day.	

1 The first day was **the easiest** because he didn't climb far.
2 The second day was _____ because he climbed for eight hours.
3 The third day was _____ because _____.
4 The fourth day was _____ because _____.
5 The fifth day was _____ because _____.
6 The sixth day was _____ because _____.
7 The seventh day was _____ because _____.
8 The eighth day was _____ because _____.
9 The ninth day was _____ because _____.

EXERCISE 6

Complete the following television broadcast by putting the adjective in brackets into the correct form.

Welcome to the Paris Motor Show, where I've been looking at all
(1) _____ (late) models, and there's no doubt in my mind that (2) _____ (impressive) car this year is this Metro 3.

As you can see, it's slightly (3) _____ (small) than many of the others on show, but inside it's (4) _____ (spacious) than it looks and, I have to admit, it's one of
(5) _____ (comfortable) cars I've ever driven. The emphasis this year is on safety and economy. So, although it's not
(6) _____ (fast) car here today, it's certainly
(7) _____ (economical). It does
(8) _____ (many) kilometres to the litre than any of the others. Changes in design have resulted in a (9) _____ (good), (10) _____ (efficient) braking system than in other models, and the introduction of power steering means it is
(11) _____ (easy) to drive. In fact, tests have shown that

this car is probably (12) _____ (safe) and (13) _____ (reliable) in the show.

The Metro 3 will cost around £9,500 and, from what I've seen of it, will definitely be (14) _____ (good) value for money in this price range.

6 ADVERBS

BIRD'S EYE BOX: Adverbs

I'm leaving **tomorrow**.	→	definite time (Exercise 1)
Think **before** you speak! We're nearly **there**. I can **never** remember his name.	→	position of adverbs of indefinite time, place and frequency (Exercises 2 and 9)
He **usually** gets home at 7.00.	→	adverbs of frequency (Exercises 3 and 9)
He spoke the language **fluently**.	→	adverbs of manner (Exercises 4, 5 and 9)
He got up **earlier** than usual. He began to walk **more quickly**.	→	comparative adverbs (Exercises 6, 7 and 9)
On the English side, Watson played **the most skilfully**. On the Irish side, O'Hara played **the best**.	→	superlative adverbs (Exercises 8 and 9)

EXERCISE 1

Make as many correct sentences as possible from boxes A, B and C. Use the prepositions in box B only where necessary.

Example: I'll have finished it ¦ in two days' time.
¦ by the end of the month.
¦ by the morning.
¦ by Tuesday.
¦ by this afternoon.

A	B	C
He's starting	in	a month ago.
I haven't seen him	at	two days' time.
I'll pay you back	since	the end of the month.
It usually arrives	on	the morning.
He should have done it	by	Tuesday(s).
She left		last week.
		this afternoon.
		today.

EXERCISE 2

Decide which is the normal position in the sentence for the words in brackets. Then write the appropriate letter (a, b or c) in the box. Sometimes more than one position is possible. The first one has been done for you.

1 I've phoned several times, but (a) there (b) is (c) no answer. (still) [c]
2 Have you (a) been (b) to the Hebrides (c) ? (ever) []
3 Ah, there it is! (a) I've been looking (b) for it (c) ! (everywhere) []
4 Cigarette?
   No thanks. I (a) have (b) put one (c) out. (just) []
5 (a) wait (b) for me (c) . (outside) []
6 (a) we don't (b) go out (c) on Saturday nights. (often) []
7 Drink this and you (a) will (b) feel better (c) . (soon) []
8 Like to have a look at the paper?
   No thanks. I (a) have (b) seen it (c) . (already) []
9 Excuse me. (a) is there (b) a garage (c) ? (near by) []
10 Don't tell me the end of the film! I (a) haven't (b) seen it (c) ! (yet) []

EXERCISE 3

Use the following notes and a suitable adverb from the box to complete the magazine article below. When there is more than one possibility, try to use as many different adverbs as possible. The first one has been done for you.

Robert Williams

1 interested in acting ever since he was a child
2 gets a part in the theatre now and then
3 is out of work sixty per cent of the time
4 helps in a friend's restaurant most of the time
5 is worried about money all the time
6 parents help him financially now and then
7 sees them only every two or three years
8 gets depressed from time to time
9 definitely wouldn't consider doing anything else

| always   continually   ever   frequently   generally   hardly ever |
| never   occasionally   often   usually   rarely   sometimes |

Life can be difficult for a young actor, as I found out when I visited Robert Williams at his home in Clapham. Robert (1) **has always** been interested in acting. If he's lucky, he (2) _____, but he (3) _____. To pay the rent he (4) _____, but he (5) _____.
His (6) _____, but as they live in New Zealand, he (7) _____. He admits that he (8) _____, but says he (9) _____.

EXERCISE 4

Complete the following table.

	ADJECTIVE	ADVERB		ADJECTIVE	ADVERB
1	careful	carefully	6	good	
2	easy		7	bad	
3	hard		8	angry	
4	thorough		9	disapproving	
5	unfriendly		10	fast	

EXERCISE 5

Choose suitable adverbs to complete the following letter of reference. You should try to use as many different adverbs as possible. The first one has been done for you.

> To Whom It May Concern
>
> Miss Thomas has worked for this company for six years and has always been an (1) **extremely** reliable and co-operative employee. She is (2) _____ well organised and does her work (3) _____ and (4) _____. She types (5) _____ and writes shorthand (6) _____. In addition, she speaks French (7) _____ and can understand German (8) _____ (9) _____. Future employers

will find that she always arrives (10) _____ and
works (11) _____ (12) _____.
   We wish her every success in her future career.

D. Martin
Managing Director

EXERCISE 6

Complete the following advertisements. The first one has been done for you.

1. Headache? You want fast relief. Paradox works **faster** than any other tablet.

2. So your batteries last a long time, do they? Try Zenox batteries. They last even _____.

3. If you think your washing powder gets your clothes thoroughly clean, then you haven't tried Dax. Dax will clean them _____.

4. I never slept very well until I drank Nightcap. Now I sleep _____ than ever before!

5. Money doesn't go very far nowadays, does it? So, shop at Savealot where your money goes _____.

6. Do you wish your photocopier was quicker, more efficient? Then change to Speedman. Speedman copies _____ and _____ than most other copiers.

EXERCISE 7

Complete the following in an appropriate way. There is often more than one acceptable answer.

Example: I'm sorry. I don't understand. Could you **say it again more slowly?**
   or   Could you **speak less quickly?**

1. If you don't hurry up, I'll miss my train. Can't you
_____?

2. If you want to pass this exam, Thomas, you'll have to
_____.

3 Children, I know you're enjoying yourselves, but I've got a terrible headache. Please can you _____?

4 Daniel, there's a police car following us! Hadn't you better _____?

5 I can't understand what's happened to the team. They've been playing pretty badly all season and last night they _____ than usual!

6 I'm sorry, but this is a very bad line, and I can't hear you. Could you _____?

EXERCISE 8

*Use the word in brackets to complete the following. Use the article (**the**) only where necessary.*

Examples: He argued **most persuasively** (persuasive).
  He argued **the most persuasively** of all the speakers (persuasive).

1 I know she thought about it (a) _____ (careful) before making a decision, and, taking everything into consideration, I think she acted (b) _____ (sensible).

2 Well, out of all the different machines to choose from, I'd say this model works (a) _____ (efficient), produces
   (b) _____ (good) copies and costs
   (c) _____ (little) to run.

3 I'm pleased to say all the ideas were received
   (a) _____ (favourable), but there's no doubt Mick's idea was received (b) _____ (enthusiastic), so that's the one we've chosen.

4 All the class has learned quite a lot, but Alfredo has definitely learned
   (a) _____ (more), which is not surprising, as he's always worked (b) _____ (hard).

5 Look, the man has written back to you (a) _____ (apologetic), explaining that there was a genuine mistake, so, under the circumstances, I think you're behaving (b) _____ (unreasonable).

EXERCISE 9

Read the following television interview. Then choose suitable adverbs to complete the discussion. There is often more than one acceptable answer. The first one has been done for you.

INTERVIEWER: My first guest this evening is the young British cyclist Ken Barclay. Ken has (1) **just** been chosen to ride in next year's *Tour de France*. Congratulations, Ken! How do you feel about it?

KEN: Thanks. Well, of course, I'm (2) _____ pleased. I (3) _____ expected to be selected.

INTERVIEWER: Which will be the most difficult part of the race for you?

KEN: Well, I'm not very good at climbing. I ride (4) _____ on flat roads. So, I don't expect to do (5) _____ in the mountains.

INTERVIEWER: You must have to do a lot of training, don't you?

KEN: Yes, of course. I train (6) _____ for about five or six hours. But (7) _____ I've been training even (8) _____ than that. But I'm still not as good as I should be! You see, it's a very long race. You have to ride (9) _____ than in most other races, and there are (10) _____ any rest days, maybe only one or two. So, it's (11) _____ tiring, too. You've got to be (12) _____ fit.

INTERVIEWER: It's a dangerous sport, too, isn't it?

KEN: Oh, yes, (13) _____! You have to ride so (14) _____ to each other that it's very easy to fall. (15) _____ the worst accident I've (16) _____ had was breaking a finger, but some riders have been (17) _____ injured. Some have even been killed.

INTERVIEWER: Well, Ken, the very best of luck in the *Tour*, and let's hope you finish the race (18) _____!

7 QUANTIFIERS

BIRD'S EYE BOX: Quantifiers

We haven't got **much** time. How **many** people are coming?	→	**much/many** (Exercises 1 and 3)
		LARGE QUANTIFIERS
He showed **a great deal of** interest. There's **plenty of** room. There are **a number of** problems.	→	**a great deal (of)/plenty (of)/a number (of)** (Exercises 2 and 3)
He's got **lots of/a lot of** ideas.	→	**a lot (of)/lots (of)** (Exercise 3)
		SMALL QUANTIFIERS
They had **a few** drinks. She's made **a little** progress.	→	**a few/a little** (Exercises 4, 5 and 8)
Few people have heard of him. She had **little** success.	→	**few/little** (Exercises 5 and 8)
There were **fewer** people than expected. He had **less** money than he thought.	→	**fewer/less** (Exercises 6 and 8)
		NEUTRAL QUANTIFIERS
Would you like **some** tea?	→	**some** in questions (Exercise 7)
I need **some** help. Have you made **any** plans yet?	→	**some/any** (Exercises 7 and 8)
He left **several** days later. She received **quite a few** offers.	→	**several/quite a few** (Exercise 8)

EXERCISE 1

Tom is talking to a friend about a party he went to. Complete the following with **much** *or* **many**. *The first one has been done for you.*

What was the party like ? Oh, not very good. There were too (1) **many** people there, so there wasn't (2) _____ room to dance or move about and talk to people. How (3) _____ people were there? About forty, I should think. Mind you, I didn't know (4) _____ of them and I'm not very good at talking to people I don't know. I didn't get there till late anyway, so, by the time I got there, there wasn't (5) _____ food left or (6) _____ drink either. I've been to one or two of her parties before, but not (7) _____. I don't think I'll go to another one. It wasn't (8) _____ fun.

EXERCISE 2

*Complete the following with **a great deal (of)**, **plenty (of)** or **a number (of)**. Sometimes more than one answer is possible.*

Example: I don't know why you think she's lonely. She's got **plenty of** friends.

1 Being a primary school teacher, she must have _____ patience.
2 _____ people have asked me the same question. I'm afraid I really don't know the answer.
3 Come on, everyone. There's _____ food, so help yourselves!
4 I've complained about it _____ times, but they still haven't done anything about it.
5 There's no need to get any more petrol. There's _____ in the tank.
6 It's kind of you to offer, but there isn't really _____ work to do.

EXERCISE 3

Complete the following dialogue by choosing words from the box below. Frequently more than one answer is possible, but you should try and use each quantifier at least once. The first one has been done for you.

| much   many   a lot (of)   lots (of)   a great deal (of) |
| a number (of)   plenty (of) |

DIRECTOR: Has there been (1) **much** response to the job advertisement?
MANAGER: Oh, yes. We've had (2) _____ applications. The only trouble is that not (3) _____ of them are really suitable. They've either got (4) _____ qualifications but not (5) _____ experience or vice versa. Take this girl, for example. She hasn't got (6) _____ qualifications, but she's had (7) _____ different jobs.

DIRECTOR: Still, sometimes experience is more important than qualifications. Anyway, we haven't got (8) _____ time, so we'll have to make a decision soon. Have you any idea how (9) _____ we'll need to interview?
MANAGER: Well, I've put (10) _____ of them aside for you to look at, and then we can make a short list.
DIRECTOR: Fine. I've got (11) _____ things to do this morning, but I should have (12) _____ time this afternoon. So perhaps we can discuss it then.
MANAGER: That suits me.

EXERCISE 4

*Complete the following weather forecast with **a few** or **a little**. The first one has been done for you.*

After a clear night, it will be a dry day in most places, though (1) **a few** areas will have (2) _____ rain in the afternoon. In the south it will be rather dull with only (3) _____ sunshine and the possibility of (4) _____ showers later in the day. In the Midlands and East Anglia there may be (5) _____ fog at first, but this should clear quickly, giving a bright day with temperatures (6) _____ degrees above zero. The cold weather over Scotland is likely to continue for (7) _____ more days, with (8) _____ snow on high ground. However, milder weather is expected by the weekend.

EXERCISE 5

*Complete the following conversations with **a few, few, a little** or **little**. The first one has been done for you.*

1 TOM: Oh, come on! Liverpool have very (a) **little** chance of winning! After all, they've lost nearly every match this season.
   MICK: I'm not so sure. They've got (b) _____ good players and, with (c) _____ bit of luck, they might just beat Rangers.

2 DIRECTOR: A very successful meeting, don't you think?
   CHAIRMAN: Very successful indeed. Just think, we've had (a) _____ arguments, (b) _____ disagreement and (c) _____ objections. In fact, we've made quite a lot of progress.

3 STUDENT: You wanted (a) _____ words with me, sir?
   PRINCIPAL: Ah, yes, Patrick. Come in. It's about your work. Now, I know this exam is of (b) _____ importance to you personally, but (c) _____ of the students have complained about your behaviour in class. I would be grateful if you could make (d) _____ more effort for the rest of the term.

EXERCISE 6

*Read the following information about two cars. Then compare the saloon with the GT using **fewer** and **less**. The first one has been done for you.*

The Saloon
1 2 doors
2 4 seats
3 Acceleration: 0–100 kms in 12 seconds
4 Petrol consumption: 20 kms to the litre
5 4 gears
6 Choice of colours: red, blue, grey
7 Extras: cigarette-lighter, radio

The GT
1 4 doors
2 6 seats
3 Acceleration: 0–100 kms in 7 seconds
4 Petrol consumption: 14 kms to the litre
5 5 gears
6 Choice of colours: red, black, silver, blue, yellow
7 Extras: cigarette-lighter, radio, cassette player, electric windows, air-conditioning

1 The saloon has **fewer** doors.
2 The saloon has _____.
3 The saloon has _____.
4 The saloon uses _____.
5 The saloon has _____.
6 There is _____.
7 There are _____.

EXERCISE 7

*Some secretaries are talking at lunchtime. Complete the following sentences with **some** or **any**. The first one has been done for you.*

1 'Thank goodness it's lunchtime! I'm starving! I didn't have **any** breakfast!'

2 'Have you got (a) _____ change, Barbara? I need (b) _____ for the coffee machine.'

3 'I'm going out. I've got (a) _____ shopping to do. We've got (b) _____ people coming for dinner and there isn't (c) _____ food in the house.'

4 'That smells nice, Pam. What is it?'
'It's home-made soup. Would you like to try _____?'

5 'Have _____ of you seen my lighter? I left it on my desk.'

6 'Oh, no! There isn't (a) _____ milk left!'
'Do you want (b) _____ of my powdered milk?'
'Thanks.'

EXERCISE 8

The actor Brian Amos is being interviewed. Complete the conversation by choosing words from the box below. Sometimes more than one answer is possible, but you should try to use each quantifier at least once. The first one has been done for you.

| a few   few   a little   little   some   any   quite a few   several |
| fewer   less |

INTERVIEWER: Now, Brian, you've been voted Actor of the Year. How do you feel about that?

BRIAN: I'm delighted, of course, but I could name (1) **quite a few** actors who are better than I am. I've just had (2) _____ more luck than they have. That's all.

INTERVIEWER: Is luck very important in the theatre, then?

BRIAN: Oh, definitely. You see, there are very (3) _____ good parts, so it's very competitive.

INTERVIEWER: Did you find it difficult at first?

BRIAN: Yes, very. It was (4) _____ months before I got my first job, and so I didn't have (5) _____ money. Then I was lucky enough to get (6) _____ small parts on television, but even then I earned very (7) _____.

INTERVIEWER: But it must be easier now that you're well known.

BRIAN: Well, of course, I have (8) _____ financial problems than I did before, but I still have to work just as hard. I mean, (9) _____ people think actors have an easy life, only working in the evenings. Well, that's quite wrong. During the day we have to rehearse new plays or look for more work, so we

	probably have (10) _____ free time than most people.
INTERVIEWER:	And have you got (11) _____ idea what you'll do next?
BRIAN:	Well, there are (12) _____ things I'm interested in doing. I've had (13) _____ offers from film directors and producers, but I haven't made (14) _____ definite plans yet.
INTERVIEWER:	Brian Amos, thank you for talking to me.

8 MODALS

BIRD'S EYE BOX: Modals

Shall I do it for you?	→	**shall, will, could** (offers, requests, suggestions, willingness) (Exercises 1 and 11)
I'd rather watch the film than the football match.	→	**would like to/prefer to/sooner/ rather** (preferences) (Exercises 2 and 11)
You'**d better** go home.	→	**had better, should, ought to** (advice/moral obligation) (Exercises 3 and 11)
Can you drive?	→	**can, could, may, might** (ability, permission, possibility) (Exercises 4, 5 and 11)
He **wasn't able to** be there.	→	**be able to, be allowed to** (ability, permission) (Exercises 5 and 11)
You **must** work harder!	→	**must, have to** (obligation) (Exercises 6 and 11)
You **needn't** do it now.	→	**mustn't, needn't, don't have to** (negative obligation/absence of obligation) (Exercises 7 and 11)
You **can't have** forgotten already!	→	**must, must have, can't, can't have** (logical conclusion) (Exercises 8 and 11)
Didn't he **use to** live near you?	→	**used to** (past habit) (Exercises 9, 10 and 11)
He **would** think about it for hours before making a decision.	→	**would** (past habit) (Exercise 10)

EXERCISE 1

Complete the following short dialogues by choosing from the boxes below. You should make combinations from A + B + D or C + D. The first one has been done for you.

A	B	D
Shall / Will / Could	I / you / we	have a look at it / stay for lunch / put the kettle on / have another piece / go to the cinema / get them / have the salt / eat out / get some stamps / show you how to use it

C: I'll

1. 'Let's have a cup of tea.'
   'Good idea. **Shall I put the kettle on?**'

2. '_____, please?'
   'Here you are. Do you want the pepper as well?'

3. 'David, there's something wrong with the iron.'
   'All right. _____ later.'

4. '_____ this evening?'
   'That's a good idea. What's on?'

5. '_____?'
   'I'd love to, but I really can't. I have to be home by 1.00.'

6. 'I'm just going down to the Post Office.'
   'Oh, _____ for me, please?'

7. 'This is a lovely cake, Jean. Did you make it yourself?'
   'Yes, I did. _____?'

8. 'I really can't work this telex machine!'
   'It's easy. _____?'

9. '_____ tonight for a change?'
   'No, I think I'd prefer to eat at home.'

10. 'Oh, dear! I've left my glasses upstairs.'
    'Don't move. _____ for you.'

EXERCISE 2

Complete the following short dialogues by putting the words provided into the correct form and choosing a suitable verb to follow. Read each dialogue carefully as you will sometimes need to use negatives. The first one has been done for you.

1 **like   sooner**
'We're going shopping this afternoon. (a) **Would** you **like to come** with us?'
    'It's nice of you to ask me, but I (b) _____ at home if you don't mind. I'm quite tired.'

2 **like   rather   prefer**
'What shall I get Harry for his birthday? Do you think he
(a) _____ something to wear or
(b) _____ he _____ money?'
    'Well, I expect he (c) _____ his own clothes, so I'd give him money.'

3 **rather   sooner**
'Shall we go to France again this year or (a) _____ you _____ somewhere else?'
    'Well, I (b) _____ anywhere too hot. I don't like too much sun.'

4 **prefer   sooner   like**
'You look very tired, dear. (a) _____ you _____ instead of going out for a meal?'
    'No, I (b) _____, but I
(c) _____ a rest before we go.'

5 **like   rather**
'Honestly, I know she earns a lot of money, but look how hard she works! I
(a) _____ her job!'
    'Nor would I. I (b) _____ less money and have more free time, wouldn't you?'

6 **prefer   like**
'Well, we can only advise you, Mr Shelley. It's really your decision.'
    'Yes, I know, but I (a) _____ a decision immediately. I (b) _____ a few days to think about it.'

EXERCISE 3

*Which of the following sentences can take **had better (not)** and which must take **should(n't)** or **ought(n't) to**? Complete the following, using **had better (not)** where possible.*

Examples: Alison doesn't feel very well, **I'd better** take her home.

I think the Government **should** spend more on education. Don't you?

1 We _____ leave quite early in the morning. The traffic's terrible.

2 You _____ give it to me. I might lose it. Give it to Edward.

3 Do you think mothers with very young children _____ go out to work?

4 _____ you _____ tell him before he finds out?

5 The question we want to discuss is '_____ violent films be shown on television?'

6 In my opinion, the police already have enough power. They _____ be given any more.

7 We _____ make too much noise or the neighbours might complain.

8 I think I _____ take an umbrella. It looks like rain.

9 _____ you _____ check the times of the train before we leave?

10 You _____ be so impatient. It's not my fault if I don't understand!

EXERCISE 4

*Complete the following, using **can('t)**, **could(n't)**, **may (not)** or **might (not)** and choosing a suitable verb from the box below. Do not use any verb more than once. There is sometimes more than one acceptable answer. The first one has been done for you.*

come	go	have	leave	read	take	turn	understand	use

1 Honestly, he spoke so fast I **couldn't understand** a word he said!

2 _____ we _____ our cases here while we have lunch?

3 I'd take a coat with you. It _____ cold later.

4 _____ I _____ your phone? Ours is out of order.

5 I'd like to go to Sally's party, but I _____ time.

6 If you don't want to drive, you _____ always _____ by train.

7 Tom's a very good pianist, even though he _____ a note of music!

8 The House of Commons was interesting, but we _____ photos, which was a pity.

EXERCISE 5

Complete the following news items by choosing from boxes A or B. There is often more than one acceptable answer. The first one has been done for you.

A
can   can't
could   couldn't
might   might not
may   may not

B	
will be won't be	
is isn't are aren't	allowed to
was wasn't were weren't	+ able to

1

Mrs Hilda Barker, who lost her eyesight five years ago (a) **can** now see again, thanks to surgeons at Moorfields Eye Hospital. Mrs Barker said, 'I (b) _____ tell you how wonderful it was when I opened my eyes and I (c) _____ see!' A hospital spokesman said, 'There is always the chance that she (d) _____ lose her sight again, but we doubt it.' Mrs Barker hopes she (e) _____ leave hospital in two weeks' time.

2

John Barratt, M. P., is looking into the case of a Vietnamese refugee who (a) _____ enter the country because his papers were not in order. 'The poor man (b) _____ speak a word of English,' said Mr Barratt, 'so he (c) _____ understand what was happening. He's obviously very worried that the Government (d) _____ let him stay here. I hope I (e) _____ do something for him, but it (f) _____ take several weeks.'

3

Two schoolgirls, who were sent home for wearing make-up, (a) _____ miss their university entrance examinations if they (b) _____ return to school next week. 'If the girls (c) _____ take these exams,' complained one parent, 'they (d) _____ go to university. I know they broke the school rules, but the headmaster is being unreasonable.' The headmaster, James Craig, said, 'The girls knew they (e) _____ wear make-up, but they did. However, if they are prepared to apologise, I (f) _____ consider letting them return.'

EXERCISE 6

Complete the following sentences by choosing the correct words (a or b) and write the appropriate letter in the box. Sometimes both answers are possible.

Example: As he's the managing director, the **a/b** attend a lot of meetings.
    (a) must   (b) has to   boxed: b

— 43 —

1 It's a really good film. You _____ go and see it.
   (a) must   (b) have to

2 Remind me to go to the bank at lunchtime. I _____ cash a cheque.
   (a) must   (b) have to

3 Richard's long-sighted. He _____ wear glasses for reading.
   (a) must   (b) has to

4 You can't go straight on. It's a one-way street. You _____ go round the market square.
   (a) must   (b) have to

5 I'm not going out for lunch. I've got some work I _____ finish.
   (a) must   (b) have to

6 I really _____ wash my hair tonight. It's filthy!
   (a) must   (b) have to

7 It's my mother's birthday on Friday. I _____ remember to get her a card.
   (a) must   (b) have to

8 Your father's already gone to bed. He _____ go to work tomorrow.
   (a) must   (b) has to

EXERCISE 7

Read the following and then complete the spaces by choosing from boxes A and B. Each phrase in box B should be used twice. The first one has been done for you.

A

mustn't
needn't
don't have to

B

do it	get up yet
drive so fast	say it again
eat it	tell the others

1 You **mustn't tell the others**. It's confidential.
2 You _____. You're not well enough.
3 You _____. I heard you the first time!
4 You _____. I've already told them.
5 You _____ if it's poisonous.
6 You _____. It's not polite!
7 You _____. We've got plenty of time.
8 You _____. It's only 5.00 a.m.

9 You _____ if it's dangerous.
10 You _____ if you don't like it.
11 You _____. There's a thirty m.p.h. speed limit.
12 You _____ if you don't want to.

EXERCISE 8

*Complete the following with **must**, **can't**, **must have** or **can't have** and the correct form of the verb in brackets. The first one has been done for you.*

1. 'Bill (a) **can't** (be) serious about giving up his job, surely?'
   'I think he is.'
   'Well, in that case, he (b) _____ (be) mad!'

2. 'Oh, you (a) _____ (know) who I mean! She's terribly famous and she's made lots of films. You (b) _____ (see) her!'

3. 'There's no answer. They (a) _____ (be) in.'
   'Don't be silly. They (b) _____ (go) out. They're expecting us. They (c) _____ (be) in the garden.'

4. 'Have the police got any idea how the man got in?'
   'Well, they say he (a) _____ (climb) through a window, as they were all closed. So they think he (b) _____ (have) a master key.'

5. 'That's Barbara over there, isn't it?'
   'No, it (a) _____ (be). That girl's much too fat.'
   'It is Barbara, you know.'
   'Well, she (b) _____ (put) on a lot of weight, then!'

6. 'My keys (a) _____ (be) here somewhere. I (b) _____ (lose) them.'
   'You (c) _____ (have) some idea where you put them, surely?'

EXERCISE 9

*Amy Cathcart has lived in the same street for fifty years. What did life use to be like? Read what she says and then complete the exercise below, using **used to** or **didn't use to**. The first one has been done for you.*

> Well, (1) it's not as friendly as in the old days, with (2) neighbours calling in on each other. (3) People don't leave their doors open any more. Perhaps it's because (4) there's more crime nowadays. I don't know. (5) The traffic's much worse, too, so (6) children can't play in the street any more. It's too dangerous. I don't know where they go instead, as (7) most mothers go out to work nowadays. Of course, (8) mothers always stayed at home when I was young. In some ways life's easier nowadays, but I miss the community feeling we used to have.

1 **It used to be more friendly.**
2 _____.
3 _____.
4 _____.
5 _____.
6 _____.
7 _____.
8 _____.

EXERCISE 10

*Which of the following sentences can take **would** and which must take **used to**? Complete the following, using **would** wherever possible, even though **used to** is also correct.*

Examples: She **used to** be a concert pianist.

   She **would** practise every day for hours.

1 Bob was such an enthusiastic photographer that he _____ spend all day trying to get the right photo.

2 Before he was transferred, Gary North _____ play for Leeds.

3 The two friends had very strong opinions and _____ argue passionately about anything they believed in.

4 On her way to work, Hilary _____ stop at the newsagent's and buy a paper to read on the train.

5 Before they opened the by-pass, the traffic _____ be much worse in the city centre.

6 In winter, the old men _____ sit in the library where it was warm.

7 I _____ like her before she got promotion and became very self-important.

8 Alan didn't get on with his mother-in-law. So, whenever she came to visit, he _____ find an excuse to go out.

EXERCISE 11

Complete the following pieces of conversation, heard at a party, with a suitable modal verb. Sometimes there may be more than one acceptable answer. The first one has been done for you.

'Are you going already?'
'Yes, we (1) **have to** take the babysitter home.'
(2) '_____ I get your coats for you?'

'Another glass of wine, Harry?'
'No, thanks. I (3) _____ have a beer this time.'
'Harry, you (4) _____ drink too much or you (5) _____ drive home!'

'Who's that man over there, talking to Peter?'
'Oh, I (6) _____ remember his name, but I think he (7) _____ work with Sheila before she changed her job.'

'You (8) _____ be Sheila's sister! You look just like her!'

'I thought Tom was coming to the party.'
'Oh, he phoned earlier to say he (9) _____ be late.'

'You (10) _____ try one of these sandwiches, Terry. They're awfully nice.'

(11) '_____ you _____ dance, Catherine?'
'Not really, if you don't mind. I (12) _____ sit here and talk.'

'It's getting awfully late, Derek. We (13) _____ go home.'
'Oh, we (14) _____ leave yet. Tomorrow's Saturday.'

(15) '_____ I open a window, Sheila? It's awfully hot in here.'
'Yes, of course. (16) _____ you manage, or (17) _____ I do it for you?'

'I (18) _____ give you a lift home if you like, Mary.'
'If you (19) _____ drop me off at the end of my road, I'd be very grateful.'

'Lovely party, Sheila. Thanks for inviting us.'
'Well, I was glad you (20) _____ come.'

9 TENSES

BIRD'S EYE BOX: Tenses

What **are** you doing? He **didn't** say anything. It**'s** made of solid gold. How long **have** you been here?	→	**be, do, have** as auxiliaries (Exercise 1)
He **comes** from Hull, but he**'s studying** electronics in London.	→	present simple, present continuous (Exercises 2, 8, 9 and 10)
Do what I tell you and **don't argue**!	→	imperative (Exercises 3, 8 and 10)
He **cut** himself while he **was shaving**. She still **hasn't come**, and we**'ve been waiting** for an hour! Everyone knew he**'d lost** his job because he**'d been cheating** the company.	→	past simple, past continuous, present perfect simple, present perfect continuous, past perfect simple, past perfect continuous (Exercises 4, 5, 8, 9 and 10)
I**'ll see** you later. What **are** you **going to do**? They**'re leaving** in the morning. The plane **lands** at 4.30.	→	**will, going to**: present continuous as a future, present simple as a future (Exercises 6, 8, 9 and 10)
We**'ll be having** dinner at 7.30, but we**'ll have finished** by 8.00. They**'ll have been going** out together for three years by the end of July.	→	future continuous, future perfect, future perfect continuous (Exercises 7 and 9)
The Queen **is to visit** Nepal in the autumn.	→	**be to** (Exercise 9)

EXERCISE 1

*Complete the following letter with the correct form of **be**, **do** or **have**. Read the letter carefully before you start, as you will sometimes need to use negatives. The first one has been done for you.*

Dear Graham,

I'm sorry to say that we (1) **are** having a disastrous holiday! To start with, the plane (2) _____ delayed for six hours, so we (3) _____ arrive until 3.00 a.m. Fortunately, the courier (4) _____ still waiting to meet us, but when we got to the hotel, we found they (5) _____ double-booked our room! So now we (6) _____ staying in another hotel, which, believe it or not, (7) _____ still being built! This means we (8) _____ woken up every morning by the workmen. Why (9) _____ it always happen to us?! It's not a very good hotel, either. The shower (10) _____ work, and yesterday, when we (11) _____ getting ready for dinner, the water supply (12) _____ cut off. I complained to the manager, but he (13) _____ seem very interested, and, of course, he (14) _____ done anything about it yet. He has a typical 'let's wait until tomorrow' attitude. (15) _____ you know what I mean?

The weather (16) _____ been pretty awful since we got here. Last Saturday we took a train to the capital. (17) _____ you ever been there? There's nothing much to see, and when we arrived we found Angela (18) _____ forgotten the traveller's cheques, so we (19) _____ speak to each other for the rest of the day! It (20) _____ raining again this morning, and, as there's nothing else to do, I (21) _____ writing a few letters. Also, we (22) _____ both had bad stomachs for the last couple of days, so we (23) _____ want to go too far from the hotel!

By the way, (24) _____ you remember to video the Cup Final for me last weekend? It (25) _____ matter if you forgot. I hear Sheffield City lost, which (26) _____ surprise me, as they (27) _____ been playing very badly recently.

> Well, we'll see you in another week and, quite honestly, we won't be sorry to come home. With the food, the weather and the hotel, I (28) _____ think we'll (29) _____ coming here again!
>
> Regards,
> *Derek*

EXERCISE 2

Complete the following dialogues by putting the verbs in brackets into the correct form. Use only the present continuous or the present simple. Where there is also an adverb in the brackets, decide the correct position in the sentence. The first one has been done for you.

1. A: How (a) **do** you **work** (work) this photocopier? I
    (b) _____ (think) I
    (c) _____ (do) something wrong.
   B: Yes, you (d) _____ (press) the wrong button. That one (e) _____ (enlarge) the copies. You
    (f) _____ (need) to press this one.
   A: Oh, yes. It (g) _____ (work) properly now. Thanks.

2. A: I (a) _____ (see) the price of petrol
    (b) _____ (go) up again.
   B: Yes, I (c) _____ (know). I
    (d) _____ (seriously consider) selling the car. It's so expensive, and we (e) _____ (not often use) it.
   A: What (f) _____ your wife _____ (think) of that idea?
   B: She (g) _____ (agree) with me. She
    (h) _____ (not like) driving anyway.

3. A: Good-morning. Is Mr Cranshaw in?
   B: Yes, he is, but he (a) _____ (see) someone at the moment. (b) he _____ (expect) you?
   A: Yes, I (c) _____ (have) an appointment with him at 10.30. My name's Phillips.

B: Ah, yes, Mr Phillips. I'm afraid we (d) _____ (run) a little late this morning, but I (e) _____ (not expect) Mr Cranshaw will be long, if you (f) _____ (not mind) waiting.

4 A: Why (a) _____ we _____ (wait)?
   B: John isn't here yet. I (b) _____ (expect) he (c) _____ (have) trouble with his car again.
   A: Oh! That car (d) _____ (always go) wrong! Well, I (e) _____ (not wait) any longer. I (f) _____ (not want) to miss the start of the match. (g) _____ you _____ (come) with me, or not?

5 A: What (a) _____ you _____ (make), Pamela? It (b) _____ (smell) really nice.
   B: Well, I (c) _____ (try) a recipe my mother-in-law gave me. It (d) _____ (sound) really easy. You (e) _____ (cut) up the meat and vegetables and then you (f) _____ (just add) a few herbs. When she (g) _____ (make) it, it (h) _____ (taste) really delicious. But I'm not sure about this. It (i) _____ (not look) quite right.

6 A: What (a) _____ you _____ (think) of that new girl, Jacqueline?
   B: Well, frankly, I (b) _____ (find) her terribly annoying. She (c) _____ (always make) silly remarks and she (d) _____ (never listen) to anything you say.
   A: I (e) _____ (know) what you (f) _____ (mean), but I (g) _____ (feel) a bit sorry for her, actually. I (h) _____ (think) she (i) _____ (try) to hide her shyness by being funny, but she (j) _____ (only succeed) in getting on everyone's nerves!

EXERCISE 3

Complete the following by selecting from the boxes below. Use the ideas in box C or make combinations from A + C or B + C. The first one has been done for you.

A	C
Do Do not Don't	tell me about it forget your key help yourselves go somewhere else turn off the electricity supply go for a walk say I'm out disturb

B
Let's

1 OK, everyone. There's plenty to eat and drink, so **do help yourselves**!
2 I'm tired of staying indoors. I need some fresh air. _____.
3 I'll be in bed when you come home, so _____.
4 It sounds terribly exciting! _____!
5 Examination in progress. _____.
6 _____ before repairing the machine.
7 I'm busy, so if anyone phones, please _____.
8 I'm fed up with going to discos! _____ for a change!

EXERCISE 4

How many meaningful and grammatically correct sentences can you make by combining the ideas in boxes A, B and C?

Example: **They were driving home when the car broke down.**

A	B	C
They were driving home He didn't know what to do He's been working here I haven't seen him We'd already left The police arrived She was keeping watch We'd been enjoying ourselves	when while since before as soon as just as by the time	the trouble started. you've been away. they began arguing. he was counting the money. he left school. the car broke down. it started to rain.

EXERCISE 5

A woman has been accused of shop-lifting. Complete the following extract from her trial by putting the verbs in brackets into the correct form. The first one has been done for you.

PROSECUTION: Mr Williams, you (1) **were** (be) the security officer on duty at Malgo Department Store on July 28th. Please tell the court what (2) _____ (happen) that afternoon.

WILLIAMS: Yes, sir. I (3) _____ (be) particularly interested in the cosmetics department, because the company (4) _____ (lose) a lot of money through shop-lifting earlier in the year. So, I (5) _____ (watch) the customers on the security screen when I (6) _____ (notice) a woman behaving rather suspiciously.

PROSECUTION: What exactly (7) _____ she _____ (do)?

WILLIAMS: Well, she (8) _____ (seem) rather nervous and she (9) _____ (keep) looking round as if she (10) _____ (want) to make sure that no one (11) _____ (watch) her.

PROSECUTION: (12) _____ you ever _____ (see) the woman before that afternoon?

WILLIAMS: No, sir. She (13) _____ (not be) one of our regular customers.

PROSECUTION: I see. Please go on.

WILLIAMS: Well, then she suddenly (14) _____ (pick) up a bottle of perfume and (15) _____ (put) it in her shopping bag.

PROSECUTION: And she (16) _____ (not pay) for the perfume, I presume?

WILLIAMS: No, sir. And then she (17) _____ (leave) the store.

PROSECUTION: So what (18) _____ you _____ (do)?

WILLIAMS: I (19) _____ (follow) her and (20) _____ (ask) her to return to the manager's office. When she (21) _____ (empty) her bag, we (22) _____ (find) that she (23) _____ (take) a lipstick and some mascara as well.

PROSECUTION: And she (24) _____ (not pay) for any of them?

WILLIAMS: No, sir.

PROSECUTION: Mr Williams, how long (25) _____ you _____ (work) at Malgo Department Store?

WILLIAMS: For about three years, sir.
PROSECUTION: And (26) _____ you _____ (catch) many shop-lifters in that time?
WILLIAMS: Quite a few, sir. Shop-lifting is a problem in any big store.
PROSECUTION: Quite. So you always know when someone is about to take goods without paying?
WILLIAMS: Not always, sir. But over the years I (27) _____ (learn) to recognise the signals.
PROSECUTION: Thank you, Mr Williams. That is all.

EXERCISE 6

Choose the best words (a, b, c or d) to complete the sentence and write the appropriate letter in the box. Sometimes more than one option is acceptable.

Example: Right. I _____ you up at 7.30, if that's convenient.
    (a) am going to pick (b) am picking (c) will pick (d) pick   [c]

1. What _____ to Sandra's party on Saturday?
   (a) are you going to wear (b) are you wearing (c) will you wear
   (d) do you wear

2. We'd better hurry up. The train _____ in half an hour.
   (a) is going to leave (b) is leaving (c) will leave (d) leaves

3. He _____ sociology at university in the autumn.
   (a) is going to study (b) is studying (c) will study (d) studies

4. I'm just going to the bank. I _____ long.
   (a) am not going to be (b) am not being (c) won't be (d) don't be

5. I've got an appointment with the dentist tomorrow. I expect he _____ something wrong. He always does!
   (a) is going to find (b) is finding (c) will find (d) finds

6. There's a good film on television tonight. What time _____?
   (a) is it going to start (b) is it starting (c) will it start
   (d) does it start

7. We _____ to the States to spend Christmas with our son.
   (a) are going to fly (b) are flying (c) will fly (d) fly

8. You've got plenty of time. The plane _____ off until 4.30.
   (a) isn't going to take (b) isn't taking (c) won't take
   (d) doesn't take

9 That really makes me angry! This time I _____ to him about it!
   (a) am going to speak   (b) am speaking   (c) will speak   (d) speak

10 If you give me that letter now, I _____ it on my way home.
   (a) am going to post   (b) am posting   (c) will post   (d) post

EXERCISE 7

*Jenny and Peter are going to drive from London to Brussels next weekend. Look at the map and their itinerary and then complete the exercise below. Use the **will be doing**, **will have done** or **will have been doing** forms of the verbs in brackets in your answers. The first one has been done for you.*

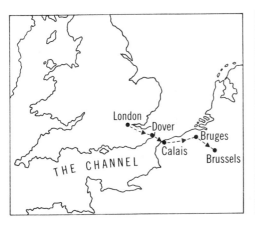

0730	Leave London
0930	Arrive in Dover
1030	Cross the Channel
1200	Arrive in Calais / Stop for lunch
1330	Leave Calais
1530	Get to Bruges
1630	Reach Brussels

1 By 0800 **they'll have left London** (leave).
2 At 0830 _____ (drive).
3 By 1000 _____ (arrive).
4 By lunchtime _____ (cross).
5 At 1300 _____ (have lunch).
6 At 1500 _____ (drive).
7 By 1545 _____ (get to).
8 By 1700 _____ (reach).
9 By the time they reach Brussels _____ (travel) for nine hours.

EXERCISE 8

Complete the following letter by putting the verbs in brackets into the correct form. Occasionally there is more than one possible answer. The first one has been done for you.

Dear Debbie,

Thanks very much for your letter, which (1) **arrived** (arrive) more than six weeks ago! I (2) _____ (mean) to reply to it for ages, but I just (3) _____ (not have) time.

As you (4) _____ (know), I (5) _____ (start) a new job at the beginning of the month and I (6) _____ (work) incredibly hard ever since. It's quite interesting, and I (7) _____ (like) my new boss, but I (8) _____ (not finish) until six o'clock and when I (9) _____ (get) home, I'm too tired to do anything! Anyway, I (10) _____ (tell) you all about it another time.

I (11) _____ (take) a week's holiday very soon and I (12) _____ (think) of coming to London the weekend after next. My sister (13) _____ (invite) me to stay with her for a few days because her husband (14) _____ (go) to France on business for a week. (15) _____ you _____ (make) any plans for that weekend? If not, (16) _____ (meet) for lunch on the Saturday or Sunday. It's ages since I last (17) _____ (see) you and I (18) _____ (have) lots to tell you. Anyway, I (19) _____ (phone) you during the week to see if you're free.

With love,
Alison

P.S. (20) _____ (give) my regards to Chris.

EXERCISE 9

*Read the following items from the **Barston Gazette**, a local newspaper. Then complete the articles by putting the verbs in brackets into the correct form. Occasionally there is more than one possible answer. The first one has been done for you.*

1

Schoolboy Saved from River

Local schoolboy Brian Walker (a) **is recovering** (recover) in hospital after falling into the River Bar. Mr Paul Bates, who (b) _____ (take) his dog for a walk at the time, (c) _____ (jump) into the water and (d) _____ (pull) the boy to safety. Brian (e) _____ (play) on the river bank when the accident (f) _____ (happen).

2

Lorries Anger Residents

Residents of Beechwood Avenue (a) _____ (protest) to the council about the number of lorries using the road. 'They (b) _____ (drive) down our road to avoid going through the High Street,' (c) _____ (complain) one resident. 'But they (d) _____ (make) so much noise that I (e) _____ (not be able) to sleep for weeks. And they (f) _____ (always break) the speed limit! One day there (g) _____ (be) a serious accident, if the council (h) _____ (not stop) them.'

3

Give Generously on Saturday!

Next Saturday, Friends of Barston Hospital (a) _____ (collect) money in the High Street to buy more equipment for the hospital. 'We (b) _____ (hope) that by the end of the day we (c) _____ (raise) at least £800,' (d) _____ (say) the organiser. 'We (e) _____ (need) a new incubator for premature babies and this money (f) _____ (help) us buy one.' At the moment the Friends (g) _____ (look) for volunteers to help on Saturday.

4

Cottage Destroyed by Fire

Police (a) _____ (think) that children accidentally (b) _____ (start) the fire that (c) _____ (burn) down an empty cottage in Woodend Lane last Sunday. Neighbours (d) _____ (call) the fire brigade, but, by the time they (e) _____ (arrive), the roof (f) _____ (fall) in. Workmen (g) _____ (now demolish) the remains of the cottage.

5

Fred Dies at 101

Barston's oldest inhabitant, Fred Whyte, (a) _____ (die) at the age of 101. Fred (b) _____ (live) in Barston since

1924 and (c) _____ (teach) at the local primary school until he (d) _____ (retire) in 1950. His funeral (e) _____ (take) place next Friday.

6

Novelist to Open Library

The popular novelist Barbara Bartlett (a) _____ (open) the new extension to Barston library next Wednesday afternoon. Miss Bartlett, who (b) _____ (write) more than twenty best-selling novels, (c) _____ (sign) copies of her latest book from three to four o'clock.

EXERCISE 10

Read the following story about a man who found a leak (a small hole in a water-pipe) in his bathroom. Then complete the story by putting the verbs in brackets into the correct form. The first one has been done for you.

Richard Barnes (1) **had just come** (just come) home from work when he (2) _____ (find) a leak in the bathroom. Water (3) _____ (drip) from the ceiling for some time, and there (4) _____ (be) a large pool of water on the floor. As soon as he (5) _____ (see) the leak, he (6) _____ (call) the plumber. The plumber's wife (7) _____ (answer). 'I'm afraid he (8) _____ (go) out an hour ago and he (9) _____ (not come) back yet. I (10) _____ (tell) him to phone you when he (11) _____ (come) in. I (12) _____ (not expect) he (13) _____ (be) long.'

Richard (14) _____ (hang) up and (15) _____ (sit) down to wait. Two hours later the phone (16) _____ (ring).

'This is the plumber. I (17) _____ (believe) you (18) _____ (call) earlier.'

'Where on earth (19) _____ you _____ (be)?' (20) _____ (demand) Richard angrily. 'I (21) _____ (wait) for two hours! What (22) _____ you _____ (do) all this time?'

'I'm terribly sorry, sir,' the plumber (23) _____ (answer) nervously. 'I (24) _____ (have) a breakdown while I (25) _____ (drive) along the motorway. I (26) _____ (only just get) home. I (27) _____ (not even have) my dinner yet. My wife (28) _____ (get) it now.'

'Well, I'm sorry about your breakdown,' (29) _____ (say) Richard in a more friendly voice. 'But (30) _____ you _____ (repair) my leak tonight or not?'

'(31) _____ (not worry), sir,' (32) _____ (reply) the plumber. 'I (33) _____ (have) my dinner and then I (34) _____ (come) straight round.'

Richard (35) _____ (put) down the receiver and (36) _____ (go) back into the bathroom. The water (37) _____ (still drip) slowly into the bowl he (38) _____ (put) under the leak. He (39) _____ (empty) the bowl again and then (40) _____ (sit) down to wait. Two hours later he (41) _____ (pick) up the receiver again. Just as he (42) _____ (dial) the number, the doorbell (43) _____ (ring).

'I'm terribly sorry, sir,' (44) _____ (say) a small, dark-haired man apologetically. 'I (45) _____ (think) I (46) _____ (have) to get a new car!'

10 UNREAL PAST

BIRD'S EYE BOX: Unreal past

It's time we **left**.	→	**it's (high) time** (Exercise 1)
I'd rather/sooner you **told** him yourself.	→	**would rather/sooner** (Exercise 2)
I **wish** I **had** more time. **If only** I **hadn't done** it.	→	**wish/if only** (Exercise 3)
Suppose someone **saw** you? **Suppose** someone **had seen** you?	→	**suppose** (Exercise 4)
You talk **as if/as though** you **didn't like** him. She acts **as if/as though** I'd done something awful!	→	**as if/as though** (Exercise 5)

EXERCISE 1

*Mary Adams is talking to her son, Gerry. Read the following and then complete the exercise below by changing the clause or sentence after each number (1, 2, etc.) so that it begins with **It's time** or **It's high time**. The first one has been done for you.*

Are you still in bed, Gerry? It's 11.30 and (1) you still haven't got up yet! What are you? A child? (2) You should grow up! It's ridiculous at your age. I don't understand you at all! (3) You don't do any work. (4) You don't earn any money. You can't expect your father to support you all your life! (5) You should find a job! We're not made of money, you know. (6) You should start to consider your father and me!

1 **It's time you got up.**   4 _____.
2 It's high time _____.   5 _____.
3 It's _____.   6 _____.

EXERCISE 2

*Use the following sentences to complete the letter below. Begin each phrase with **I'd rather** or **I'd sooner**. The first one has been done for you.*

1. I don't want anyone else to know.
2. Please don't say anything to anyone.
3. Think about it carefully.
4. Please be honest and tell me.
5. Do what you think is right.
6. Please don't phone me at work.

MINISTRY OF DEFENCE

Memorandum

To: Major Reginald Armstrong

From: Sir Frederick Halt

Date: 2 April 19—

Just a note to remind you of our recent conversation and the offer I made you. (1) **I'd rather no one knew** about it for the time being. It's not exactly top secret, but you know what the newspapers are like. So, (2) _____ for the moment, not even your wife. Please don't feel you have to make a decision immediately. (3) _____ first of all. And don't feel you have to accept just because we're old friends. If you're not interested (4) _____. I've always respected your strength of character, Reggie, so (5) _____.

Incidentally, (6) _____. You never know who might be listening. Call me at home when you're ready.

Freddie

EXERCISE 3

*Paul's at an informal party. Use the following information to complete Paul's thoughts. Begin each sentence with **I wish** or **If only**. The first one has been done.*

1 He doesn't know anyone.
2 He's shy.
3 He's sorry he came to the party.
4 He feels nervous.
5 He's sorry he didn't stay at home.
6 He's sorry he's put on a suit.
7 He doesn't have much self-confidence.
8 He can't dance.

1 **I wish I knew someone.**

EXERCISE 4

*Read the following television announcement and then complete the dialogue below. Begin each phrase with **Suppose**. The first one has been done for you.*

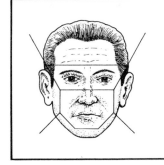

The police have issued this photofit picture of the man they wish to question about the recent attacks in Brentford. (1) Do you recognise this man? (2) Do you know who he is? (3) Is he a friend of yours? (4) Were you in the area when the attacks took place? (5) Did you hear or see anything suspicious? Anyone who (6) has any information and can help the police should phone Brentford 701. This man is dangerous. (7) He has attacked before.

ANNE: (1) **Suppose you recognised that man,** what would you do?
DEREK: What do you mean?
ANNE: Well, (2) _____ or, even worse, (3) _____, would you tell the police?
DEREK: But I don't know him, so the question isn't relevant, is it?
ANNE: Well, all right. But just (4) _____ when the attacks took place. (5) _____, would you phone that number?
DEREK: I don't know and I'm not really interested.
ANNE: OK. But (6) _____ and _____ to catch the man, surely it would be your duty to tell them?
DEREK: Well, possibly.
ANNE: What do you mean 'possibly'! Just (7) _____ you instead of those old ladies, what then?
DEREK: Attacked me? Well, that would be different, wouldn't it?

EXERCISE 5

Complete the sentences by choosing from boxes A, B and C below and putting the verb into the correct form. The first one has been done for you.

A	B	C
as if	live	a fortune
as though	be	a crime
	have	something terrible
	commit	the company
	win	a palace
	say	a complete idiot
	run	all the time in the world

1 You know we're in a terrible hurry, but you act **as if we had all the time in the world**!

2 He's only an office clerk, but he behaves _____ he _____!

3 OK, I made a mistake, but there's no need to treat me _____ I _____!

— 64 —

4 She only won £100, but she talks _____ she _____!

5 I only said I didn't like it. There's no need to look at me _____ I _____!

6 It's only a small two-bedroomed house, but she talks _____ she _____!

7 Look, I'm sorry I forgot your birthday, but do stop behaving _____ I _____!

11 TO + INFINITIVE/INFINITIVE WITHOUT TO

BIRD'S EYE BOX: To + infinitive/infinitive without to

Would you like **something to eat?**	→	object + **to** + infinitive (Exercises 1 and 8)
It's too **hot to drink.**	→	adjective + **to** + infinitive (Exercises 2, 3 and 8)
I don't know **how to thank** you.	→	question word + **to** + infinitive (Exercise 4)
I've come **to see** the manager.	→	**to** + infinitive (purpose) (Exercise 5)
I've **decided to change** my job.	→	verbs followed by **to** + infinitive (Exercise 8)
Let me **speak!** **Make** him **be** quiet!	→	**let/make** + infinitive (Exercises 6 and 8)
I **heard** him **come** in.	→	verbs of perception + infinitive (Exercises 7 and 8)
You **mustn't make** a noise.	→	modals + infinitive (Exercise 8)

EXERCISE 1

Choose a suitable verb to complete the following. Sometimes more than one verb would be appropriate. The first one has been done for you.

1 Sandra! I've got something **to tell** you!

2 Sorry, I'll have to go now. I've got a train _____.

3 Excuse me, sir. There's a Mr Thatcher _____ you.

4 I'm afraid I can't come out tonight. I've got too much homework _____.

5 I'll have to buy a new dress. We're going to a party on Saturday and I've got nothing _____.

6 At the moment I'm staying with friends, but I'm looking for a flat _____.

7 It was so embarrassing! They asked me to make a speech, but I couldn't think of anything _____!

8 Do I have to make a decision now, or can I have a few days _____ about it?

EXERCISE 2

The following letter was published in a newspaper. Complete the letter by choosing the appropriate verb from the box below. Do not use any verb more than once. The first one has been done for you.

be   employ   give   have   learn   let   read   say   work

Dear Sir,

I was not at all surprised (1) **to read** in the paper that there are now more unemployed young people than ever before. If I were a boss, I'd be very reluctant (2) _____ anyone under twenty-five. What can school-leavers offer an employer? They're too young (3) _____ any experience, and, I'm sorry (4) _____, most of them are too lazy (5) _____ hard! They are quite happy (6) _____ the State look after them, because the State is foolish enough (7) _____ them money for doing nothing!

Yours faithfully,

A. J. Williams

EXERCISE 3

Join each of the following pairs of sentences to make one sentence and then complete the letter below. The first one has been done for you.

1. I read the letter from A. J. Williams. I was extremely angry.
2. He says that young people are lazy. This is stupid.
3. They don't have any experience. They aren't old enough.
4. Employers don't offer them jobs. Employers are unwilling.
5. Young people learn. They are quick.
6. They work hard. They are keen.
7. You see young people out of work. This is very sad.
8. The young won't look for jobs. They'll be too depressed.

Dear Sir,

(1) I was **extremely angry to read the letter from A. J. Williams**. (2) It is _____.
Of course (3) they _____, but how can they get experience if (4) employers _____?
(5) Young people _____ and
(6) they _____. I think
(7) it is _____.
If the situation doesn't change soon, (8) the young _____.

Yours faithfully,

E. F. Bonner

EXERCISE 4

David was driving his car one evening when he had a puncture. He is telling his friend about it. Complete the following by choosing the correct question word from the box on the left and the appropriate verb from the box on the right. Do not use any verb more than once. The first one has been done for you.

where	which	what		ask	change	do	go	join
who	how	whether		leave	say	stay	tell	

Well, I knew I had to do something, but I didn't know (1) **what to do**. I suppose most people can change a wheel themselves, but I had no idea (2) _____ it. You see, I'm not very mechanical. So I thought I'd better ask someone to help me, but I couldn't decide (3) _____. I mean, you feel so stupid! Anyway, I decided I'd have to go to a garage, but, not knowing the area very well, I wasn't sure (4) _____. It's my own fault, I know. I should have joined one of those motoring organisations, like the A A or the R A C. The trouble is, I could never decide (5) _____. I mean, they both have their advantages and disadvantages, don't they? Anyway, there I was on a Saturday evening, wondering (6) _____ in the car or look for a garage, when a young woman stopped and asked if she could help. Imagine my surprise when, in a few minutes, she'd changed the wheel for me! Well, I was speechless! I just didn't know (7) _____!

EXERCISE 5

Yesterday Linda made a list of the various things she had to do. Read the list and then complete the sentences below. Sometimes more than one answer is acceptable.

1. Times of trains to Oxford?
2. Library – books back.
3. Marino's – table for two on Saturday.
4. Post Office – stamps.
5. Hairdresser's – appointment Friday p.m.
6. Bank – £50.
7. Dental appointment, 10.30 Tuesday – cancel.
8. Anne – come to lunch on Sunday?

Example: Doctor's – prescription.
          She went to the doctor's **to collect a prescription**.

1. She phoned the station _____ the times of the trains to Oxford.
2. She went to the _____.
3. She phoned _____.

4 She went _____.
5 She rang _____.
6 She went _____.
7 She phoned _____.
8 She rang _____.

EXERCISE 6

*Read the following conversation. Decide first if you should use **let** or **make** and then choose the appropriate verb from the box below to complete the conversation. Do not use any verb more than once. The first one has been done for you.*

| ache   do   drink   eat   feel   have   know   laugh   make   think |

PENNY: I hear you spent a week at a health farm. What was it like?

HELEN: Absolutely dreadful! They (1) **make you do** exercises from morning till night and they don't (2) _____ you _____ anything except for grapefruit. It was worse than being in prison!

PENNY: But did it do you any good?

HELEN: Oh yes! I lost twelve kilos and I feel much better! In fact, I'm going back next month.

PENNY: Oh, Helen, you do (3) _____ me _____! You're so funny! I'm sure it wasn't as bad as all that!

HELEN: No, I suppose not. To be honest, it was quite enjoyable, especially the sauna. That (4) _____ you _____ marvellous! But, if you're not used to doing anything energetic, the exercises really (5) _____ your legs _____ by the end of the day.

PENNY: I've often wondered what health farms are like.

HELEN: Well, I've got a booklet about it at home. I'll (6) _____ you _____ a look at it, if you like. If you're interested, why don't you come with me next month?

PENNY: Well, I might, but (7) _____ me _____ about it first. It sounds like hard work! Oh! All right! I'll have a look at the booklet and then I'll (8) _____ you _____ later!

EXERCISE 7

A sports reporter interviewed several people about an incident involving two players, Foreman and Sherriff, in a football match. He wrote down statements made by each of them. Join each of the following pairs of sentences to make one sentence and then complete the newspaper report that follows. The first one has been done for you.

TURNER:	1	Foreman deliberately knocked Sherriff down. I saw him.
FOREMAN:	2	Sherriff fell down. I noticed him.
	3	The referee blew his whistle. I didn't hear him.
CARSTON:	4	Sherriff tripped over. I saw that.
	5	But did Foreman touch him? I didn't notice.
SHERRIFF:	6	Someone shouted. I heard him.
	7	Someone pushed me from behind. I felt it.
FOOTBALL SUPPORTER:	8	Foreman's played lots of matches. I've watched him.
	9	He's never fouled before. At least, I've never seen him.

Football Star Sent Off

There was a storm of protest yesterday after referee Sam Turner sent off top player Tim Foreman for fouling against Bob Sherriff. After the match Turner said, (1) '**I saw Foreman deliberately knock Sherriff down.** I blew my whistle, but Foreman ignored it, so I showed him the red card.' Foreman angrily denied this, saying, (2) 'I _____, but I never touched him. I carried on playing because (3) _____.' Team-mate Willie Carston agreed with Foreman when he said, 'I shouted at Foreman to pass me the ball. Then (4) _____, but (5) _____.' Sherriff refused to speak to reporters, but his manager said, (6) 'Sherriff _____ and then (7) he _____. There was definitely a foul.' Foreman supporters found it hard to believe. As one supporter put it, (8) '_____, but (9) _____.'

EXERCISE 8

Ron Blakelock has been dismissed from his job for hitting one of the managers, Mr Cowley. The other workers are on strike because they believe Mr Cowley started the trouble. Complete the following discussion by using the verb in brackets as an infinitive with or without to. *The first one has been done for you.*

TOM: Now, I've spoken to the Managing Director, and he seems (1) **to be** (be) ready (2) _____ (listen) to our side of the story. In fact, he's offered (3) _____ (talk) to us, but only if we agree (4) _____ (go) back to work immediately. I said I'd let him (5) _____ (know) our decision after this meeting. Well, have you got anything (6) _____ (say)?

BERT: Yes, I have. I'm not returning to work until he promises (7) _____ (give) Ron his job back. And no one can (8) _____ (make) me! After all, that's why we're on strike, isn't it?

TOM: No one's going to make you (9) _____ (do) anything, Bert. But you must (10) _____ (remember) that it's a difficult situation. Everyone saw Ron (11) _____ (hit) Mr Cowley. There's no doubt about that. The question is why he hit him. We hope (12) _____ (show) that it was Mr Cowley's own fault. But we can't (13) _____ (do) that if the management refuses (14) _____ (discuss) it with us, can we?

DAVE: Tom's right, Bert. Frankly, I think we should (15) _____ (do) what the Managing Director says. It's not very sensible (16) _____ (stay) on strike under the circumstances. It won't help Ron (17) _____ (get) his job back, will it?

BERT: I still don't like it. We all know what Mr Cowley said to Ron.

TOM: Yes, but no one heard him (18) _____ (say) it, did they? It's Ron's word against Mr Cowley's. Look, let's (19) _____ (have) a vote. Anyone who wishes (20) _____ (continue) the strike, put up your hand. Well, it looks as if the majority wants (21) _____ (return) to work. What about you, Bert? What have you decided (22) _____ (do)?

BERT: You needn't (23) _____ (worry). I intend (24) _____ (accept) the majority decision.

TOM: Good. Now, I've got a lot of things (25) _____ (do) first, but I'll arrange for us (26) _____ (meet) the Managing Director as soon as possible. In the meantime, I'll tell him he can (27) _____ (expect) (28) _____ (see) us back at work tomorrow.

12 GERUND

BIRD'S EYE BOX: Gerund

Cycling is good exercise.	→	as a subject (Exercises 1, 2 and 6)
What do you fancy **doing**? You promised **to help** me.	→	gerund or **to** + infinitive (Exercises 3 and 6)
He left without **saying** goodbye.	→	after prepositions (Exercises 4 and 6)
He's **trying to start** the car. (Aim) Has he **tried checking** the oil? (Method)	→	verbs followed by **to** + infinitive or gerund, with different meanings (Exercises 5 and 6)

EXERCISE 1

Join the two sentences to make one sentence, beginning with a gerund.

Example: She's a nurse. It's hard work.
   Being a nurse is hard work.
   or **Nursing is hard work.**

1 She looks after young children. It's very tiring.
2 He didn't get the job. It depressed him.
3 They share a flat. This sometimes causes arguments.
4 She's a teacher. It requires a lot of patience.
5 He never goes out. That must be boring.
6 He doesn't have any friends. This must make him lonely.

EXERCISE 2

Read the politician's speech and write down his solutions to the problems. The first one has been done for you.

> 'Today we are faced with many problems, both social and economic. What are we, the Government, going to do about them? (1) First of all, we are going to create new jobs. This will reduce unemployment. (2) Then we must export more goods, which will help the economy. Of course, the future of the country is in the hands of the young, (3) so we intend to train more teachers, and this will raise the level of education. (4) We must also provide more entertainment for young people. This will keep them out of trouble. (5) In addition, we plan to cut taxation, and this will help the lower-paid workers. (6) And, finally, we are going to employ more policemen, which will make our streets safer.'

1 <u>**Creating more jobs will reduce unemployment.**</u>
2 _____.
3 _____.
4 _____.
5 _____.
6 _____.

EXERCISE 3

Complete the dialogue with the correct form of the verb in brackets (gerund or to + infinitive). The first one has been done for you.

MANAGER: I thought you ought to know, sir, I've decided (1) **<u>to give</u>** (give) in my notice. I hope (2) _____ (leave) at the end of the month.

DIRECTOR: Thank you for (3) _____ (let) me know, Dennis, but I can't help (4) _____ (wonder) why you want (5) _____ (leave). You've been with this company for ten years now, so you can't dislike (6) _____ (work) here, surely?

MANAGER: Oh, certainly not, sir. I've really enjoyed (7) _____ (be) here. It's just . . . well, it's difficult.

DIRECTOR: Yes? Go on.

MANAGER: Well, I didn't want (8) _____ (say) this, sir, but I just can't stand (9) _____ (work) with Mr Mitchell, the deputy manager. If I don't leave soon, I'll end up (10) _____ (do) something I might regret.

DIRECTOR: I see. Would you mind (11) _____ (tell) me exactly what the problem is?
MANAGER: Well, I don't mean (12) _____ (be) unfair to him. He's young and ambitious, but he's full of these new ideas. He keeps (13) _____ (try) to change things.
DIRECTOR: Is that such a bad idea, Dennis?
MANAGER: It is when the men refuse (14) _____ (work) with him, sir. It's making my life impossible. So, I don't feel like (15) _____ (stay) with the company under the circumstances.
DIRECTOR: I understand you (16) _____ (feel) this way, Dennis, and I appreciate you (17) _____ (tell) me about it. However, I have offered (18) _____ (transfer) Mr Mitchell to another branch, and I'm expecting his answer this afternoon. I can't promise anything, but if he agrees (19) _____ (go), perhaps you'd consider (20) _____ (stay) with the company?
MANAGER: Yes, of course I would, sir.

EXERCISE 4

Read through the news items and fill in the spaces with a suitable word or phrase. The first one has been done for you.

And here is a round-up of the news in brief.

Two men escaped from Durham jail early this morning by (1) **climbing** a wall. Both men were serving five years for (2) _____ an elderly man.

Police are looking for a hit-and-run driver who drove off without (3) _____ after (4) _____ a young woman. Police are interested in (5) _____ anyone who saw the accident.

Boxing champion Steve Goddard appeared in court today, accused of (6) _____. He was found not guilty. Goddard spoke to reporters before (7) _____ and said that he was now looking forward to (8) _____.

Pop star Scott Turner plans to retire after his next European tour. He said today he was tired of (9) _____ and wanted to spend more time with his family instead of (10) _____.

British racing driver Bob Nicolas flew home last night after (11) _____ the Brazilian Grand Prix. His car developed engine trouble during the race, and he had difficulty in (12) _____.

An Essex grandmother, Mrs Maude Williams, celebrated her 100th birthday today by (13) _____ Concorde. She was nervous of (14) _____ before the flight, but, on (15) _____ Heathrow Airport, she said she'd had a wonderful time and thanked everyone for (16) _____.

And, finally, a young man who took his pet snake to a party ended up (17) _____ the night at the local police station. Paul Rimmer, twenty-six, said, 'I was worried about (18) _____ the snake at home because of the cold. So I put it into a box and left it in a bedroom. It was all right until someone insisted on (19) _____ the box and the snake escaped. That's when the police were called.' Mr Rimmer apologised for (20) _____ and was later allowed to go home.

EXERCISE 5

Choose the correct words (a or b) to complete the sentence and write the letter in the box provided.

Example: Graham wants to drive to Spain, but I'd prefer _____.
　　　　(a) to fly　(b) flying　　　　　　　　　　　　　　　　　　　　|a|

1. I hope she remembers _____ him the message when she sees him tonight. It's important.
   (a) to give　(b) giving

2. It was such a funny story, I couldn't stop _____!
   (a) to laugh　(b) laughing

3. If you're not getting a good picture on your television, try _____ the aerial.
   (a) to adjust　(b) adjusting

4. She began her career as a model and then she went on _____ films.
   (a) to make　(b) making

5. Now, you remember _____, but do you remember anything else about the accident?
   (a) to skid　(b) skidding

6. I'd hate _____ into trouble with the police. Wouldn't you?
   (a) to get　(b) getting

7   It was a very good flight. We only stopped once _____ in Kuwait.
    (a) to refuel   (b) refuelling

8   Although the policeman shouted, 'Stop!', the man went on _____.
    (a) to run   (b) running

9   I hate _____ to get up early. Don't you?
    (a) to have   (b) having

10 Please make a little less noise. I'm trying _____.
    (a) to concentrate   (b) concentrating

EXERCISE 6

Complete the letter with the correct form of the verb in brackets (gerund or to + infinitive). The first one has been done for you.

Dear Carol,

Many apologies for not (1) **replying** (reply) to your letter earlier, but I've been awfully busy. Thanks very much for (2) _____ (invite) me to stay with you over the bank holiday weekend. Of course, I'd love (3) _____ (come).

However, instead of (4) _____ (drive) as I usually do, I've decided (5) _____ (come) by train, as I don't fancy (6) _____ (sit) in a traffic jam for hours! As you know, (7) _____ (drive) on a bank holiday is always murder!

I'm planning (8) _____ (catch) the 8.45 from Waterloo Station, which gets in about eleven o'clock. Please don't worry about (9) _____ (meet) me at the station. It isn't far to your house, so I don't mind (10) _____ (walk). In fact, after (11) _____ (sit) for a couple of hours on a crowded train, I'll enjoy the fresh air!

By the way, I'd like (12) _____ (bring) something for the children. I was thinking of (13) _____ (get) them each a book. Do they still like (14) _____ (read), or would they prefer (15) _____ (have) something else? What do you think?

I must say, I'm really looking forward to (16) _____ (see) you again and to (17) _____ (hear) all your news. I've got some interesting news I want (18) _____ (tell) you, but it'll have (19) _____ (wait) until I see you. Anyway, do remember (20) _____ (let) me know about the children.

See you soon.

Love,

Christine

13 PARTICIPLES

BIRD'S EYE BOX: Participles

It was a **worrying** situation. We were all very **worried**.	→	present and past participles used as adjectives (Exercises 1, 2 and 9)
Students **starting** on Monday should arrive by 8.30. Fees **paid** in advance are not refundable.	→	present and past participles to introduce an adjectival phrase (Exercises 3 and 9)
Sitting in the front row, we had an excellent view.	→	present participle to introduce an adverbial phrase (Exercises 4 and 9)
Opening the door, the cat came in.	→	misrelated participles (Exercise 5)
I noticed him **coming** along the road.	→	present participle after verbs of perception (Exercises 6 and 7)
Having visited the museum, we decided to have lunch in the park.	→	present perfect participle to introduce an adverbial phrase (Exercises 8 and 9)

EXERCISE 1

Complete the following newspaper headlines with the correct form of the verb in brackets.

Examples: Police recover **stolen** (steal) jewellery in Scotland.

Frazer wins championship after **exciting** (excite) match.

1 _____ (fall) trees block Birmingham–Wolverhampton road.
2 Pilot tells of _____ (amaze) escape.
3 Government policy blamed for _____ (rise) prices.
4 Football star in hospital with _____ (break) leg.
5 Police search for _____ (miss) child.

6 _____ (burst) water-pipes cause flooding in central London.
7 _____ (worry) parents demand meeting with Education Minister.
8 Queen returns home after _____ (exhaust) tour.

EXERCISE 2

Complete the following newspaper article by putting a circle round the correct word in brackets. The first one has been done for you.

FILM REVIEW

When I first saw his work, I thought David Lennox seemed a (1) (promising)/ promised) young director. So, I was (2) (interesting/ interested) to see his latest film, *Vermilion*. I was not (3) (disappointing/disappointed). The story is very (4) (exciting/ excited) the special effects are (5) (astonishing/astonished), and I was most (6) (impressing/impressed) by the photography. Unfortunately, the same cannot be said of *Tell Me Another*, Freddie Dash's latest film. Advertised as 'an original comedy', it is neither original nor (7) (amusing/amused). In fact, some of the jokes are so bad as to be almost (8) (embarrassing/ embarrassed). I was not (9) (surprising/surprised) that most of the audience appeared totally (10) (boring/bored) by the end, as the story is most (11) (confusing/ confused). I am sorry to say that it is a most (12) (disappointing/ disappointed) film.

EXERCISE 3

Complete the following notices and announcements by choosing a verb from the box below and putting it into the correct form (present or past participle). Do not use any verb more than once.

| arrive buy damage leave meet wait wear |

Example: Passengers **wishing** to smoke should sit at the rear of the bus.

1 The train _____ at platform two is the 10.43 to Reading.
2 Goods _____ in transit should be returned to the manufacturer.
3 Cars _____ in a no-parking zone will be removed.
4 Any guest not _____ a tie will be asked to leave.
5 Clothes _____ in the sale cannot be changed.
6 Friends and relatives _____ passengers from New Delhi are advised that flight BA763 has been delayed.

EXERCISE 4

Read the following extract from a story. Then choose a suitable verb and put it in the correct form to complete the passage. The first one has been done for you.

(1) **Moving** carefully and not (2) _____ a sound, Douglas slowly made his way towards the window. (3) _____ through a gap between the curtains, he could see the three men. The fat one, Wiseman, stood by the fireplace, (4) _____ a cigar and (5) _____ excitedly to Petersson, the Norwegian. Petersson appeared to be listening intently, (6) _____ from time to time as if Wiseman had said something funny. The third man, Wescott, sat on the sofa, (7) _____ the paper, not (8) _____ the other two. Suddenly, the door opened and a fourth man came in, (9) _____ a large suitcase, which he put down on the table. As Douglas stood (10) _____ the four men in the room, he heard a sound behind him. (11) _____ round, he could just see in the darkness the shape of a man only a few metres away. (12) _____ his gun out of his jacket, Douglas stepped into the shadow of a tree and waited.

EXERCISE 5

Read the following sentences and decide which are acceptable and which are not. Put a tick (√) or a cross (X) in the appropriate box and then correct those you find unacceptable.

Example: Answering the phone, the toast burnt. ☒
While I was answering the phone, the toast burnt.

1 Driving along the road, a car pulled out in front of me. ☐
2 Reading the book a second time, I understood it better. ☐
3 Hidden in the wood, the police found a body. ☐
4 Looking left and right, the traffic slowed down and she crossed the road. ☐
5 Exhausted by the journey, he went straight to bed. ☐
6 Walking across the golf course, a golf ball hit him. ☐

EXERCISE 6

A film director is talking to some actors about the scene they are going to film. Use the notes below to complete his directions. The first one has been done for you.

1	watch/children/play	5	see/shark/come
2	look at/some girls/sunbathe	6	hear/Rita/shout
3	see/something/move	7	feel/surfboard/rock
4	notice/Dave/windsurf	8	hear/Dave/scream

OK. Now, the next scene is on the beach, and we want to create a nice, peaceful atmosphere. Rita, you're (1) **watching the children playing** in the water, and Peter, you're (2) _____ farther along the beach, through your binoculars. OK? Suddenly, Rita, you (3) _____ through the water. You borrow Peter's binoculars to see more clearly, and then you realise it's a shark. At the same time, you (4) _____ near by. That's when you start shouting. Right? Now, Dave, you don't (5) _____ towards you and you're too far away to (6) _____. The first time you realise something is wrong is when you (7) _____. You lose your balance and fall in. The scene finishes with the reaction of the people on the beach when they (8) _____. Clear? Right, quiet, everybody.

EXERCISE 7

*You spent the night in a house where strange things happened. Use the ideas below to make sentences about what you **saw, heard** and **felt**.*

Examples: Someone screamed.
 I heard someone scream.

 A figure was dancing in the garden.
 I saw a figure dancing in the garden.

1 Someone was crying in the next room.
2 A cold hand touched me.
3 Something was floating in the air above my head.
4 A door slammed suddenly.
5 A white face appeared and then disappeared.
6 Something was crawling up my arm.
7 The wind was howling outside.
8 Someone tapped me on the shoulder.

EXERCISE 8

Read the following speech by the prosecution at a murder trial. Then choose a suitable verb and put it in the correct form to complete the speech. The first one has been done for you.

Ladies and gentlemen of the jury, I intend to prove to you that the defendant, Michael Perkins, cold-bloodedly decided to kill Penelope Hennessy for money, and that, (1) **having made** that decision, he set about planning exactly how to kill her. I will show that, (2) _____ the murder in detail, he carried it out on the night of October 26th, when he shot Mrs Hennessy through the heart. I will produce evidence to show that,

(3) _____ Mrs Hennessy, he disposed of the body in the New Forest and that, (4) _____ the body, he drove to Lymington, where he threw the gun in the sea. (5) _____ the gun, he drove back to the house to remove any evidence of the crime.

(6) _____ sure that there was nothing to connect him with Mrs Hennessy's disappearance, he took several thousand pounds from the safe and hid it in the churchyard at Lyndhurst. (7) _____ the money, he returned to his own house. So far, he had committed the perfect crime. But, (8) _____ the perfect crime, he became careless and began to make mistakes. I now call the first witness for the prosecution.

EXERCISE 9

Complete the sentences with the correct form of the verb in brackets. The first one has been done for you.

1. I found it difficult to follow the serial, **having missed** (miss) the first episode.

2. _____ (annoy) by the constant interruptions, the Minister refused to continue, _____ (demand) that the trouble-makers leave.

3. Anyone _____ (travel) without a ticket may be fined up to £100.

4. She cut her foot on a piece of _____ (break) glass, half _____ (hide) in the sand.

5. _____ (realise) he'd missed the bus, Patrick began to walk home, _____ (hope) another bus would come before long.

6. _____ (take) the machine to pieces, Alan found he couldn't put it together again.

7. The river, _____ (swell) by the heavy rain, burst its banks and flooded the _____ (surround) countryside.

8 _____ (lie) in bed, _____ (worry) and _____ (depress), Sarah started to think once again about the problem.

9 Students _____ (want) to take the exam should give their names to the Principal by Friday.

10 She didn't want to hear the story again, _____ (hear) it all before.

14 THE PASSIVE

BIRD'S EYE BOX: The Passive

He **was asked** to leave. She**'s been given** promotion.	→	different tenses of the passive (Exercises 1, 2, 3 and 8)
He was attacked **by a madman**. He was attacked **with an axe**.	→	by or with + agent (Exercise 3)
It **shouldn't be allowed**! It **must be used** with care.	→	modal passives (Exercises 4, 5 and 8)
The money **is to be given** to charity.	→	passive infinitive (Exercises 6 and 7)

EXERCISE 1

Complete the following by choosing from boxes A + C or A + B + C. Use each verb once only. The first one has been done for you.

A	B	C
is/are was/were has/have had	going to be being been	changed delayed held up kept offered pulled down repaired used warned

1 All flights from Gatwick **have been delayed** because of the weather.

2 Sorry we're late. We _____ in the traffic.

3 Why can't you go down Station Road? _____ the road _____?

4 I really can't sympathise with Graham. He knew what would happen if he did it again, as he _____ before.

5 Is the dialling code for Orpington still 66, or _____ the number _____?

6 I intended to go to the car-wash on the way home, but when I got there it _____, and I didn't have time to wait.

7 You won't find the encyclopaedias in here. They _____ in the reference library.

8 You can't blame Michael for leaving. I understand he _____ a far better job.

9 I hear the old primary school _____ soon. Apparently, they want to build a block of flats on the land.

EXERCISE 2

Complete the following news items by putting the verb in brackets into the correct form. The first one has been done for you.

1 Two men (a) **are being questioned** (question) at Marylebone Police Station tonight in connection with last week's armed robbery in Luton, in which £25,000 (b) _____ (steal) from a Securicor van. Another man (c) _____ already _____ (arrest) for the crime.

2 Four people (a) _____ (take) to hospital after a fire at their home in Tottenham early this morning. They (b) _____ (send) home after treatment for minor burns. Police believe the fire (c) _____ (start) deliberately.

3 Disc jockey Paul Asherton (a) _____ (ban) from driving for two years. The court (b) _____ (tell) that it was the third time Asherton (c) _____ (stop) for speeding in six months. Asherton admitted driving at more than 125 m.p.h.

4 Missing schoolgirl Sheila Patterson, aged eleven, (a) _____ (find) alive and well in Leicester. Sheila, who disappeared two days ago, said she had left home to join a circus. Her parents are travelling to Leicester tonight. Meanwhile, Sheila (b) _____ (look) after at Leicester Police Station.

5   Lorry-driver Albert Whittaker had a lucky escape this afternoon when a concrete block, which (a) _____ (load) on to his lorry, fell off and landed inches from his feet. Mr Whittaker (b) _____ (treat) for shock.

EXERCISE 3

*Complete the second sentence so that it means the same as the first, using **by** or **with** only where necessary.*

Example: The police believe that someone used a master key to open the door.
           The police believe that the **door was opened with a master key**.

1   Adrian Holt, the well-known composer, is writing the music.
    The music _____.

2   Apparently, someone used a knife to kill her.
    Apparently, she _____.

3   The police have arrested a 39-year-old mother of three for shop-lifting.
    A 39-year-old _____.

4   Ice on the road almost certainly caused the accident.
    The _____.

5   I haven't got my car at the moment. The garage is repairing it.
    I haven't got my car at the moment. It _____.

6   The supermarket manager was afraid that someone had injected poison into some of the food.
    The supermarket manager was afraid that some of _____.

EXERCISE 4

Use the following sentences to write notices in the boxes below. The first one has been done for you.

1   'You must keep dogs on a lead.'

2   'You should collect prescriptions before midday.'

Dogs must be kept on a lead.	

3 'We will arrest shop-lifters.'

4 'You can borrow tennis-rackets on request.'

5 'You may not take reference books out of the library.'

6 'You must not remove these instructions.'

EXERCISE 5

Use the following to complete the extract from a radio programme below. The first one has been done for you.

1 We have to do something.
2 What can we do?
3 We could solve the problem.
4 We have to improve the public transport system.
5 We ought to reduce fares.
6 The Government should provide more money.
7 It would encourage people to leave their cars at home.
8 We need to introduce higher car-park charges.
9 We ought to employ more traffic wardens.
10 It would discourage drivers.
11 Will they do anything about the problem?
12 We must find a solution quickly.

London in the rush-hour! Everyone complains about it, don't they? And everyone agrees that (1) **something has to be done**. But (2) _____ about the endless traffic jams, the late trains and the overcrowded buses? We've been out to ask people in the street how they think (3) _____. Nearly everyone feels that (4) _____ and that (5) _____. To do this, they say that (6) _____, and then (7) _____. Other people feel that (8) _____ and (9) _____ so that (10) _____ from taking their cars into the city centre. But (11) _____ in the near future? We hope so, because (12) _____. Otherwise, one day soon, London's traffic will come to a complete standstill.

EXERCISE 6

Use the following sentences to write instructions in the boxes below. The first one has been done for you.

1   'Dilute this in water.'

To be diluted in water.

2   'Take these after meals.'

3   'Do not give to children under five.'

4   'Use only with soft contact lenses.'

5   'Do not spray near eyes or mouth.'

6   'Do not use on broken or sensitive skin.'

EXERCISE 7

Complete the following newspaper reports by choosing a suitable verb from the box below and putting it into the correct form. Do not use any verb more than once. The first one has been done for you.

build   give   increase   lead   open   return   take over

1

The Government is to set up an inquiry into the Mortlake train crash. The inquiry **is to be led** by the Minister of Transport, Frank Vine.

2

Two firemen, who saved the life of a sixteen-year-old girl, _____ a medal for bravery.

3

Buffers, the fast-food chain, _____ by the American supermarket Sellwell.

4

British Rail announced today that fares _____ _____ by five per cent from April.

5

In an agreement between the British and Italian governments, the Venetian Statues, at present in the British Museum, _____ to Italy.

6

Steadfast Manor, the home of Lord and Lady Steadfast, _____ to the public in June.

EXERCISE 8

Read the following extract from an adventure story. Then complete the extract by putting the verbs in brackets into the correct form. There may sometimes be more than one possible answer. The first one has been done for you.

Jake felt sure that the secret plans (1) **were hidden** (hide) somewhere in the room. He began searching carefully. Behind a picture on the wall he found a small metal safe. 'They (2) _____ (keep) in here,' he thought. Suddenly, he (3) _____ (push) violently from behind. He fell, hitting his head on the stone floor, and everything went black.

When he came round, he found that he (4) _____ (take) to a small room. His hands and feet (5) _____ (tie) with rope and he felt as if he (6) _____ (drug). He also had the strange feeling that he (7) _____ (watch). A few minutes later the door (8) _____ (unlock), and two men walked into the room. Jake immediately recognised one of them. It was Boris Mariovitch, the mad scientist!

'So, my friend,' said Boris, smiling coldly, 'what made you think the plans (9) _____ (keep) in the safe? You fool! They (10) _____ (hide) where no one will ever find them!'

'What are you going to do with him?' asked the second man, pointing at Jake.

'Him? Nothing for the moment. No doubt he (11) _____ (kill) in the morning!'

The two men left. The door slammed shut and (12) _____ (lock) from the outside. Jake looked desperately round the room. The door (13) _____ (make) of metal and (14) _____ (not break). The windows (15) _____ (not open) from the inside. What was he going to do? There was no escape! Jake (16) _____ (trap)!

15 QUESTION TAGS

BIRD'S EYE BOX: Question tags

He isn't very old, **is he?**	→	positive tags (Exercises 1, 2, 3 and 4)
You've been to Spain, **haven't you?**	→	negative tags (Exercises 1, 2, 3 and 4)
They must be very rich, **mustn't they?**	→	modal tags (Exercises 1, 2, 3 and 4)
You locked the door, **didn't you?** (falling)	→	intonation in question tags (Exercise 4)
You locked the door, **didn't you?** (rising)		

EXERCISE 1

Complete the following with the correct question tags.

Examples: You won't be long, **will you?**

  Nobody saw you, **did they?**

1 He's got a very good job, _____?
2 Well, you'd better tell me about it, _____?
3 I couldn't borrow your dictionary, _____?
4 I am right, _____?
5 That wasn't a very diplomatic thing to say, _____?
6 You'll be home early tonight, _____?
7 Everyone's gone home now, _____?
8 No one really likes him, _____?
9 You'd like to see it, _____?

EXERCISE 2

Mr Hardwick, a driving instructor, is giving a driving lesson to seventeen-year-old Gary. Complete the following dialogue with the correct question tags. The first one has been done for you.

INSTRUCTOR: Now, you remember what you learned last lesson, (1) **don't you?**

GARY: Yes, of course. Start the engine, into first gear, and we're off. That was all right, (2) _____?

INSTRUCTOR: Not really. You didn't indicate, (3) _____?

GARY: Oh, sorry, I forgot. Still, it doesn't really matter, (4) _____?

INSTRUCTOR: That's where you're wrong, Gary. I'm afraid it does matter.

GARY: Well, I can't be expected to remember everything, (5) _____? It's only my third lesson, after all.

INSTRUCTOR: OK, Gary. Anyway, watch your speed. You're going too fast.

GARY: But I'm only doing thirty-five m.p.h!

INSTRUCTOR: I know, but this is a built-up area, (6) _____? And there's a thirty m.p.h. speed limit.

GARY: But look at everyone else. They're all going faster than thirty m.p.h., (7) _____?

INSTRUCTOR: That doesn't make any difference. You haven't passed your test yet, (8) _____? Now, turn right at the next corner and – Gary, be careful!

GARY: Oh! I shouldn't have done that, (9) _____?

INSTRUCTOR: No, you certainly shouldn't have! You just weren't concentrating, (10) _____? Now, for goodness sake, pay attention!

GARY: You don't really like teaching me to drive, (11) _____, Mr Hardwick?

INSTRUCTOR: It's not a question of liking or disliking, Gary. It's my job. But if you want to pass the test, you'll just have to learn to concentrate, (12) _____? Now, let's try again.

EXERCISE 3

How many logical and grammatically correct sentences can you make from the following table?

Example: **You have got the keys, haven't you?**

You Patrick They Everyone We It	have will must is were might are would	(not)	have missed the train here got the keys be very nice paid the bill tell her thinking come late		have will must is were might are would	(not)	he? we? you? it? they?

EXERCISE 4

Complete the following with correct question tags. Look at the intonation marks and write in the box which meaning (a, b or c) is probably being expressed.

> a You expect agreement.
> b You are not sure.
> c You are showing surprise.

1 It's Tuesday, **isn't it?**   `a`

2 It was terribly crowded, _____? ☐

3 You didn't really say that, _____? ☐

4 You do like it, _____? ☐

5 It is Tuesday, _____? ☐

6 He doesn't really want the job, _____? ☐

7 I did give you the keys, _____? ☐

8 You haven't finished already, _____? ☐

9 You can see what I mean, _____? ☐

10 You wouldn't honestly do that, _____? ☐

16 CONDITIONALS

BIRD'S EYE BOX: Conditionals

I'll send you a card **if** you **give** me your address.	→	**first conditional** (Exercises 1, 2, 7, 10 and 11)
		CONDITIONAL LINKING WORDS
Supposing he doesn't like it?	→	**supposing, provided that, unless, in case, as long as, so long as** (Exercises 3, 4, 7 and 11)
If I knew where he was, **I'd (would) tell** you.	→	**second conditional** (Exercises 5, 6, 7, 10 and 11)
If he'd (had) been more careful, he **wouldn't have broken** it.	→	**third conditional** (Exercises 8, 9, 10 and 11)

EXERCISE 1

Complete the following pieces of conversation, overheard in a shop, by putting the verbs in brackets into the correct form.

Example: 'If you **leave** (leave) it with me now, it **won't take** (not take) more than a couple of days to repair.'

1 'If you _____ (wait) a minute, sir, I _____ (see) if the manager _____ (be) free.'

2 'If it _____ (not fit), madam, _____ (bring) it back and we _____ (change) it.'

3 '_____ I _____ (get) any discount if I _____ (pay) cash?'

4 'If you _____ (give) me your phone number, sir, we _____ (let) you know when it _____ (arrive).'

5 'How long _____ it _____ (take) if you _____ (order) one for me?'

6 'If you _____ (not see) what you _____ (want), sir, just _____ (ask) one of the assistants.'

EXERCISE 2

Some workers are demonstrating outside their factory. Use their demands to decide what they actually say to the managers and then complete the exercise below. The first one has been done for you.

1.
PAY US MORE MONEY OR WE GO ON STRIKE!

2.
GIVE US LONGER HOLIDAYS OR WE DON'T COME TO WORK!

3.
DON'T SHORTEN OUR LUNCH-BREAK OR WE WALK OUT!

4.
IMPROVE SAFETY STANDARDS OR WE STOP WORK!

5.
PROVIDE BETTER WORKING CONDITIONS OR WE DON'T DO OVERTIME!

6.
INTRODUCE A SHORTER WORKING WEEK OR WE COMPLAIN TO THE UNION!

1 If you don't pay us more money, we'll go on strike!
2 _____!
3 _____!
4 _____!
5 _____!
6 _____!

EXERCISE 3

The managers of the factory are considering the workers' demands. Complete the following sentences by choosing words from the box below. Use each one once only. (Occasionally there is more than one possibility.) The first one has been done for you.

> provided (that)   supposing   as long as   so long as   unless   in case

1 We'll pay them more money **so long as** they work harder.

2 We won't give them longer holidays _____ they promise to be more productive.

3 We won't shorten their lunch-break _____ they agree to start earlier.

4 We'll have to improve safety standards _____ someone has an accident.

5 We'll consider providing better working conditions _____ we have enough money.

6 _____ we introduce a shorter working week, how will we make a profit?

EXERCISE 4

Think of a suitable way to complete the second half of the dialogues.

Example: 'Do you think Patrick has much chance of passing the exam?'
'Not unless **he works harder**.'

1 'We don't need to take a map, do we?'
   'But supposing _____?'

2 'Can I borrow the car?'
   'Yes, so long as _____.'

3 'Do you think I should send it registered post?'
   'It might be a good idea, just in case _____.'

4 'So, you're thinking of buying that second-hand car?'
   'Well, as long as _____.'

5 'I hear you're planning to go camping next weekend.'
   'We hope to, provided that _____.'

6 'Do you think we'll still catch the train?'
   'Well, we won't unless _____.'

EXERCISE 5

Arthur Rainer has a lot of bad habits, which he should give up, but it's probably too late for him to change. Use the ideas to complete the exercise below, explaining why he should change his habits. The first one has been done for you.

1 Give up smoking and be healthier!
2 Go on a diet and lose weight!
3 Take some exercise and get fit!
4 Stop drinking and live longer!
5 Eat the right food and feel better!
6 Take care of your health and enjoy life more!

1 **If he gave up smoking, he'd be healthier.**
2 _____.
3 _____.
4 _____.
5 _____.
6 _____.

EXERCISE 6

Complete the following radio programme by putting the verbs in brackets into the correct form. The first one has been done for you.

INTERVIEWER: Welcome once again to our weekly programme in which we ask the questions 'If you (1) **were** (be) alone on a tropical island for a month, what two items (2) _____ you _____ (choose) to take with you and why?' My two guests today are racing driver Paul Bartlett and journalist Anna Spall. Paul?

PAUL: Well, I think I (3) _____ (get) very bored on this island if I (4) _____ (not have) anything to do. So, I (5) _____ (take) a knife and a ball of string. Then I (6) _____ (be able) to make useful things to catch food and, maybe, build some kind of house to live in.

INTERVIEWER: (7) _____ you _____ (try) to escape from the island?

PAUL: If I (8) _____ (manage) to make a boat, I think I (9) _____ (try).

INTERVIEWER: Anna, what about you?

ANNA: Well, I definitely (10) _____ (not try) to escape! I'm totally impractical. So, if I (11) _____ (try) to make anything, I'm

	sure it (12) _____ (fall) to pieces very quickly! No, if I (13) _____ (have) to spend a month on this island, I (14) _____ _____ (want) to have a good book and a pair of sunglasses!
PAUL:	But how (15) _____ you _____ (catch) things to eat if you (16) _____ (not have) any tools?
ANNA:	Oh, I expect there (17) _____ (be) plenty of fruit on the island. And I'm sure it (18) _____ _____ (not hurt) me if I (19) _____ (not eat) meat or fish for a month.
INTERVIEWER:	(20) _____ either of you _____ (be) lonely?
PAUL:	Yes, definitely. I (21) _____ (find) it very difficult if I (22) _____ (not speak) to anyone for a month.
ANNA:	I think I (23) _____ (enjoy) the peace and quiet at first, but after a couple of weeks, yes, I (24) _____ (begin) to feel lonely.
INTERVIEWER:	Paul and Anna, thank you very much.

EXERCISE 7

Complete the clauses in box A by joining each one with a suitable clause from box B to give a logical and grammatically correct sentence. The first one has been done for you.

A	B
1 If he phones while I'm out 2 I wouldn't say it 3 Supposing we rented a car 4 I'll tell you what he said 5 In case you're home before me 6 If you paid more attention 7 You can have the room for as long as you like 8 I don't mind you having a party	so long as you promise not to tell anyone. provided you pay the rent on time! please take a message. I'll give you the spare key. unless it were true. as long as you don't make too much noise. would you be prepared to share the driving? you'd know what I was talking about!

1 **If he phones while I'm out, please take a message.**
2 _____.
3 _____.
4 _____.
5 _____.
6 _____.
7 _____.
8 _____.

EXERCISE 8

Three drivers are involved in an accident. Read what they say and then complete their statements to the police. The first one has been done for you.

Key
C = Cortina
F = Fiesta
J = Jaguar

CORTINA DRIVER: 1 He didn't use his headlights. That's why I didn't see him.
                  2 I didn't see him. That's why I pulled out.

FIESTA DRIVER: 3 He didn't look carefully. That's why he didn't see me.
                  4 He pulled out in front of me. That's why I had to brake suddenly.
                  5 The Jaguar was so close behind me. That's why the driver wasn't able to stop.

JAGUAR DRIVER: 6 The driver in front braked suddenly. That's why I hit him.
                  7 I wanted to overtake him. That's why I was so close behind him.
                  8 He was such a slow driver. That's why I wanted to overtake him.

These are the statements the drivers made to the police. (Don't forget that some of them are negative.)

CORTINA DRIVER: 1 **If he'd used his headlights, I would have seen him.**
                  2 _____.

FIESTA DRIVER: 3 _____.

	4 _____.
	5 _____.
JAGUAR DRIVER:	6 _____.
	7 _____.
	8 _____.

EXERCISE 9

Read the following news items and then complete what the people say. There is often more than one acceptable answer. The first one has been done for you.

1

An elderly woman was reunited with the son she had not seen for twenty years after recognising his photograph in a national newspaper. 'It was pure chance,' said Mrs Vera Hemmings. '**If I hadn't recognised his photo, we'd never have met again**!'

2

Part of a school roof blew off in high winds yesterday and landed inches from people waiting in a bus queue. Mrs Hilda Vale, fifty-nine, said 'We were terribly lucky.
_____
_____,'

3

Two yachtsmen were rescued last night after getting into difficulty in heavy seas. Coastguards criticised the two men for not listening to the weather reports. 'These people make me very angry,' said John Smythe, a coastguard,
'_____
_____,'

4

Middle-weight boxing champion Ally Frazer lost the world title last night when he was knocked out in round six. His manager said, 'He's been working very hard recently. He's tired and his reactions aren't as fast as usual.
_____
_____,'

5

Doreen Brooker lost her chance of winning £10,000 in prize money when her husband admitted forgetting to post her entry form. 'I'm not speaking to him,' said Doreen yesterday,
'_____
_____,'

6

Tommy Mangold lost his job at a car factory last week after making an unfortunate remark about his boss's wife. 'The trouble with Tommy is that he never thinks before he speaks,' said his mother.
'_____
_____,'

EXERCISE 10

It's two o'clock in the morning. Roger and Diana have just come back from a party. Complete the following dialogue by putting the verbs in brackets into the correct form. The first one has been done for you.

ROGER: Where's your key?

DIANA: What do you mean? You've got a key, haven't you?

ROGER: (1) If I **had got** (get) mine, I **wouldn't need** (not need) yours, would I?

DIANA: No, but I haven't got mine.

ROGER: But I told you to bring it.

DIANA: No, you didn't.

ROGER: Yes, I did. (2) If you _____ (listen), you _____ (hear) me.

DIANA: Well, I don't remember you telling me. Anyway, I couldn't find it.

ROGER: You mean you've lost it again?

DIANA: Not really. It's at home somewhere. (3) I _____ (have) time to look for it if we _____ (not leave) in such a hurry.

ROGER: That's not the point. (4) If you _____ (be) more organised, you _____ (keep on) losing it in the first place!

DIANA: That's not fair! I don't keep on losing it. Anyway, what are we going to do now? We haven't got a key.

ROGER: I don't know. I suppose I'll have to break a window.

DIANA: You can't do that! (5) If the neighbours _____ (hear) you, they _____ (think) we're burglars!

ROGER: All right, then. There's a small window open in the bathroom. (6) If you _____ (stand) on my shoulders, you _____ (be) able to reach it and then you can climb in.

DIANA: I'm not going to stand on your shoulders. I might fall off!

ROGER: Don't be silly! (7) If I _____ (hold) your legs, you _____ (be) quite safe.

DIANA: I still don't like it.

ROGER: Look. (8) I _____ (climb) in myself if I _____ (can) get through the window, but I can't. I'm too big. You'll have to do it.

DIANA: (9) But if someone _____ (see) me, they _____ (call) the police!

ROGER: For goodness sake! (10) It _____ (make) things a lot easier if you _____ (not worry) about other people! Now, are you ready?

DIANA: OK.

ROGER: All right?

DIANA: (11) If you _____ (move) a bit closer, I _____ (be) able to reach. Oh! Not so fast! Roger! Oh!!

ROGER: Now look what you've done! You've put your foot through the window!

DIANA: Roger, there's something I've got to tell you!

ROGER: Honestly, can't you do anything right! (12) If you _____ (not be) so careless, you _____ (break) it!

DIANA: Roger, listen! I hate to tell you, but this isn't our house!

EXERCISE 11

Use your own ideas to complete the following.

Example: You'd get a better photo **if you used a flash**.

1 If the weather improves, _____.
2 If I knew the answer, _____.
3 Take a message _____.
4 If you'd asked me first, _____.
5 Unless she works harder, _____.
6 He wouldn't sell his car _____.
7 Provided that you feel well enough, _____.
8 If I'd known you were coming, _____.
9 If you went to bed earlier, _____.
10 It wouldn't have happened _____.

17 INDIRECT (REPORTED) SPEECH

BIRD'S EYE BOX: Indirect (reported) speech

'I'm leaving on Friday.' **He says (that) he's leaving on Friday.**	→	introduced by present tense (Exercise 1)
'I'm leaving on Friday.' **He said (that) he was leaving on Friday.**	→	introduced by past tense (Exercises 2, 4 and 8)
'Can I give you a lift?' She **offered** to give them a lift.	→	verbs used to report speech (Exercise 3)
'I'll see you tomorrow.' He said (that) he would see her **the next/following** day.	→	time words in reported speech (Exercises 4 and 8)
'Are you going to the party?' **She asked me if/whether I was going to the party.** 'When does it start?' **She asked me when it started.**	→	reported questions (Exercises 5 and 8)
'What shall I do?' **She asked me what to do.** **She asked me what she should do.**	→	reported questions with **to** + infinitive or modals (Exercise 6)
'Relax!' **He told her to relax.** **He told her (that) she should relax.** 'Don't worry!' **He told her not to worry.** **He told her (that) she shouldn't worry.**	→	reported imperative (Exercises 7 and 8)

EXERCISE 1

Read the postcard and then complete the dialogue below. It is not necessary to repeat 'He says' every time. The first one has been done for you.

Am staying with friends in California.
1) Having a wonderful time!
2) The weather's superb!
3) Have been to the Grand Canyon.
4) Hope to have a trip to Mexico.
5) Wish I could stay longer, but it's too expensive.
6) Coming back at the end of the month.

Regards,
Donald

Mr and Mrs R. Benfield,
27 The Avenue,
Shoreham,
Sussex,
ENGLAND.

PENNY: Who's the postcard from, Richard?
RICHARD: Donald. **He says (that) he's staying with friends in California.**
PENNY: How lovely!
RICHARD: Yes. (1) He says _____.
PENNY: I'm sure he is.
RICHARD: (2) _____.
PENNY: And?
RICHARD: (3) _____.
PENNY: Lucky Donald!
RICHARD: And, listen to this! (4) _____.
PENNY: How exciting!
RICHARD: (5) _____.
PENNY: How long is he staying there?
RICHARD: (6) _____.

EXERCISE 2

Read both interviews and then complete the newspaper report below. The first one has been done for you.

> INTERVIEWER: As Minister of Education, what do you think of the teachers' demand for a ten per cent pay rise?
>
> MINISTER: (1) Frankly, I have little sympathy for the teachers. (2) They are extremely lucky to have a short working day and long holidays. (3) The Government is not prepared to pay them more for doing nothing. (4) The Teachers' Union must accept that fact. (5) If they go on strike, they will be acting totally irresponsibly.

> REPORTER: As leader of the Teachers' Union, what is your reaction to the Minister's remarks?
>
> LEADER OF THE TEACHERS' UNION: (6) I am extremely angry at the Minister's remarks. (7) Teachers are hard-working, responsible people. (8) When they go home, they cannot relax because they have to mark books and prepare lessons. (9) I have been teaching for twenty years, and during that time the pay and conditions have gone down. (10) The Minister has no idea what he's talking about and should resign!

Minister Unsympathetic Towards Teachers

In a television interview last night, the Minister of Education (1) **said (that) he had little sympathy for the teachers**.

(2) He said _____.

(3) _____.

(4) _____.

(5) _____.

When asked to comment on the Minister's remarks, Tom Bollard, leader of the Teachers' Union, said (6) _____.

(7) _____.

(8) _____.

(9) _____.

(10) _____.

EXERCISE 3

Decide which would be the most suitable reporting verb from the box below to report each of the following sentences. The first one has been done for you.

> admit   advise   agree   announce   apologise   demand   offer   promise   suggest   thank   threaten   warn

1 'I want to know where you've been!' **demand**
2 'I'm terribly sorry I'm late.' _____
3 'I'll carry that case for you if you like.' _____
4 'Don't touch that switch. It's dangerous.' _____
5 'Well, if I were you, I'd see a doctor about it.' _____
6 'It was very kind of you to look after the baby for me. I'm very grateful.' _____
7 'We've decided to get married.' _____
8 'Well, why don't we go by train?' _____
9 'I really will pay you back tomorrow. Honestly!' _____
10 'All right, I was breaking the speed limit.' _____
11 'If you don't stop doing that immediately, I'll tell your father!' _____
12 'Yes, you're right. It is difficult.' _____

Now change each of the sentences into reported speech, using the correct reporting verb. You can choose which pronouns you want to use. The first one has been done for you.

1 **He demanded to know where she had been.**
2 _____.
3 _____.
4 _____.
5 _____.
6 _____.
7 _____.
8 _____.
9 _____.
10 _____.
11 _____.
12 _____.

EXERCISE 4

Read the following telephone conversation and then complete the letter below. The first one has been done for you.

'Sundridge Electrics. Can I help you?'
'I'd like to order a Bosch fridge-freezer.'
'I'm afraid (1) we sold the last one yesterday and (2) we haven't any more in stock now. But (3) we're expecting a delivery later on today. (4) They'll be here about three o'clock this afternoon. If you like, (5) I'll phone you and (6) we'll deliver one tomorrow.'

Dear Sir,

Two weeks ago I telephoned your shop to order a Bosch fridge-freezer. The assistant I spoke to told me (1) **that you had sold the last one the day before** and (2) that _____. However, he informed me (3) that _____ and (4) that _____. He then said (5) that _____ and (6) that _____. Since then I have heard nothing more. Would you kindly let me know if these fridge-freezers are now in stock.

Yours faithfully,

William Johnson

EXERCISE 5

Recently you had an interview at an employment agency. Below are the questions you were asked. Read the questions and then complete the exercise that follows.

1. What experience have you had?
2. Can you type, write shorthand and use a telex machine?
3. Have you got any qualifications?
4. Why did you leave your last job?

> 5 How long have you been looking for another job?
> 6 Do you want to work in an office again?
> 7 Are you looking for a full-time or a part-time job?
> 8 When can you start work?

Example: Have you worked before?
She asked me if/whether I had/(I'd) worked before.

What are you interested in doing?
She asked me what I was interested in doing.

1 First of all, she asked me _____.

2 Then _____.

3 And then _____.

4 Next _____.

5 And after that _____.

6 Then _____.

7 And then _____.

8 Finally _____.

EXERCISE 6

Sheila runs an advice column in a weekly magazine. Read the following letters and then complete the exercise below.

1

I have to make a speech at my daughter's wedding. What shall I say?

Derek

2

I want to complain about the postal service. Who should I write to?

Valerie

3

I'm going to my husband's office party. What should I wear?

Sylvia

4

My son is having problems learning to read. How can I help him?

Jennifer

5

I need some legal advice, but I can't afford a solicitor. Where shall I go?

David

6

My daughter can't stop biting her nails. How can I stop her?

Margaret

Example:

> My life is being made miserable by my noisy neighbours. What can I do?
>
> Paul

Paul asked her what to do about his noisy neighbours.
or **Paul asked her what he could do about his noisy neighbours.**

1 Derek _____ .
2 Valerie _____ .
3 Sylvia _____ .
4 Jennifer _____ .
5 David _____ .
6 Margaret _____ .

EXERCISE 7

Tim is very unhappy with his landlady. Read what the landlady says and then complete the dialogue below.

1 Stay in your room after dinner!
2 Eat your meals in the kitchen, not the dining-room!
3 Don't bring your friends to the house!
4 Don't use the telephone!
5 Take your shoes off when you come indoors!
6 Don't make a noise after nine o'clock!
7 Don't use the bathroom after 8.00 p.m!
8 Smoke in the garden, not the house!

Example: 'Take your washing to the launderette!'
She told me to take my washing to the launderette.
or **She told me (that) I should/must take my washing to the launderette.**

'Don't use my washing machine!'
She told me not to use her washing machine.
or **She told me (that) I shouldn't/couldn't use her washing machine.**

TIM: I must find somewhere else to live. My landlady's impossible!
BOB: Why?
TIM: She's so unfriendly. You know, she told me (1) _____ .
BOB: Really?
TIM: Yes, and she (2) _____ .
BOB: You mean, by yourself?
TIM: Yes. But that's not all. (3) _____ .
BOB: She sounds awful!

TIM: She is. The day I arrived, (4) _____.
BOB: Oh, dear!
TIM: And (5) _____.
BOB: Your shoes!
TIM: Yes! Then (6) _____.
BOB: Incredible!
TIM: But listen to this! (7) _____.
BOB: I don't believe it!
TIM: It's true! And, finally, (8) _____.
BOB: Well, I'm not surprised you want to move!

EXERCISE 8

Read the following extract from a board meeting of **Discoverer Lines**, *a shipping company. Then complete the minutes of the meeting below. The first one has been done for you.*

DIRECTOR: Right. (1) There are two ships we have to discuss this morning: the *Magellan* and the *Columbus*. (2) Mr McManus, is there any more news about the *Columbus*?

MR MCMANUS: (3) I had another telex from the captain yesterday. (4) The ship's still in Sydney Harbour and can't be unloaded because of the dockers' strike.

MR WATES: (5) Could the crew on the *Columbus* unload the ship themselves?

MR MCMANUS: No, (6) it's out of the question. (7) The Union would stop every ship in the company!

DIRECTOR: Well, (8) let me know as soon as you have any news, Mr McManus. Now, (9) I understand there's a problem with the *Magellan*. (10) What do you know about it, Mr Greaves?

MR GREAVES: (11) The *Magellan* broke down in the Mediterranean two days ago. (12) We're going to take the ship into Malta for repairs.

DIRECTOR: (13) How long will the repairs take?

MR GREAVES: (14) They shouldn't take longer than two or three days, but we may have to wait for spare parts.

DIRECTOR: (15) How much will the repairs cost, Mr Wates?

MR WATES: (16) I've got an estimate for $20,000, but that doesn't include the port charges.

DIRECTOR: (17) Are you planning supervise the repairs yourself, Mr Greaves?

MR GREAVES: (18) Yes. My flight to Malta leaves tomorrow morning.

Discoverer Lines

Minutes of meeting held on Tuesday, 29 March

1. The Director **said (that) there were two ships they had to discuss that morning: the *Magellan* and the *Columbus*.**
2. He asked Mr McManus _____.
3. Mr McManus _____.
4. He _____.
5. Mr Wates _____.
6. Mr McManus _____.
7. He _____.
8. The Director _____.
9. He _____.
10. He _____.
11. Mr Greaves _____.
12. He _____.
13. The Director _____.
14. Mr Greaves _____.
15. The Director _____.
16. Mr Wates _____.
17. The Director _____.
18. Mr Greaves _____.

18 PREPOSITIONS

BIRD'S EYE BOX: Prepositions

Wait for me **outside** the cinema.	→	place (Exercises 1, 2, 7 and 8)
He worked **from** 9.00 **to** 5.00.	→	time (Exercises 3, 4, 7 and 8)
Everyone is here **except** Terry.	→	other prepositions, prepositional phrases (Exercises 5, 7 and 8)
There's nothing to **worry about**.	→	verb + preposition (Exercises 6, 7 and 8)

EXERCISE 1

Use the picture to help you complete the second part of the short dialogues. Choose a suitable preposition from the box below, but do not use any preposition more than once. The first one has been done for you.

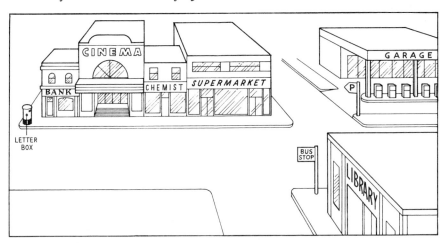

across   behind   between   in   near   next to   on   opposite   outside

1. 'Excuse me. Is there a car-park near here?'
   'Yes, there's one **behind the supermarket**.'

2. 'I wonder where I can change some money.'
   'I think there's a bank _____.'

3. 'Excuse me. I'm looking for a chemist's.'
   'Well, the nearest one is _____.'

4. 'Is there anywhere I can post a letter?'
   'Yes, there's a letter-box _____.'

5. 'I'd like to join the library, if there is one.'
   'Oh, yes, there's a library _____.'

6. 'Do you know where I can catch a bus to Harwich?'
   'Yes, the bus stop's _____.'

EXERCISE 2

Use the map to complete the notice using suitable prepositions. The clues you need are in the map. Occasionally there may be more than one correct answer. The first one has been done for you.

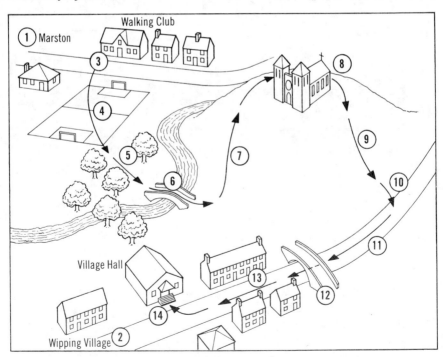

Marston Walking Club

There will be an eight-mile walk on Saturday afternoon (1) **from** Marston
(2) _____ Wipping Village. Walkers should meet
(3) _____ the club at two o'clock. The route is as follows. Go
(4) _____ the playing field, (5) _____ Woyden's
Wood and (6) _____ the bridge. Then walk
(7) _____ Hollis Hill, (8) _____ the church and
(9) _____ the hill again (10) _____ the main road.
Go (11) _____ the main road, (12) _____ the bridge
and (13) _____ the centre of Wipping Village. The walk will
finish (14) _____ the village hall. Anyone interested should
sign below.

EXERCISE 3

Complete the following shop notices with the correct preposition. The first one has been done for you.

1

Sale starts **on** Monday!

2

Closed for lunch _____ 1.00 and 2.00 p.m.

3

Late night shopping. Open _____ 8.00 p.m. _____ Thursdays.

4

Closing-down sale. Everything must go _____ the end of the week.

5

Gone for lunch. Back _____ two o'clock.

6

New Sellalot Supermarket opening _____ January!

7

Havstock will be open _____ 9.00 p.m. _____ Sales Week!

8

Open _____ 9.00 a.m. _____ 5.30 p.m.

EXERCISE 4

A member of parliament is talking to his secretary. Complete the following dialogue with the correct prepositions. The first one has been done for you.

M.P.: Right, Simon, what's the programme?

SIMON: Rather busy, I'm afraid, sir. There's a meeting tomorrow (1) <u>at</u> nine o'clock, which will probably go on (2) _____ lunchtime. Then (3) _____ lunch you've got an appointment with the Prime Minister. She's expecting you (4) _____ 2.15 and 2.30. Incidentally, the Foreign Secretary would like a word with you sometime (5) _____ the afternoon.

M.P.: The Foreign Secretary? But I thought he was flying to Paris (6) _____ the morning.

SIMON: He was, sir, but that visit's been cancelled because of the French elections. He's now going (7) _____ July instead, but no one knows exactly when.

M.P.: Oh, I see. What else?

SIMON: Well, (8) _____ Thursday you've got another meeting, which is scheduled to last (9) _____ 10.00 a.m. (10) _____ 12.00 p.m. Oh, and I almost forgot, the Home Secretary wants to see you (11) _____ the meeting starts. He said it wouldn't take long.

M.P.: I wonder what he wants.

SIMON: I think it's something to do with your visit to Manchester (12) _____ the 23rd.

M.P.: Oh, right. Any news from Sir Harold yet?

SIMON: Nothing definite, sir. I phoned his secretary earlier and, apparently, Sir Harold's been out of the country (13) _____ the last few days. I said you had to have an answer (14) _____ Friday at the latest, and he's promised to let you know (15) _____ twenty-four hours.

M.P.: I see.

SIMON: Oh, and one last thing, sir. The television people have been waiting to see you (16) _____ three o'clock.

M.P.: What do they want?

SIMON: Well, if you remember, you're doing a party political broadcast (17) _____ two days' time.

M.P.: Am I? Good heavens, I'd completely forgotten about it! Show them in immediately. This is important!

EXERCISE 5

Use the word or words in brackets to complete the second sentence so that it means the same as the first.

Example: The only person who didn't come to the party was Jane. (apart from)
Everyone came to the party apart from Jane.

1. She used a knife to open the parcel.
   She opened _____. (with)

2. The Labour Party believes that nuclear weapons are wrong.
   The Labour Party is _____. (against)

3. He was in pain, but he managed to finish the race.
   He managed to _____. (in spite of)

4. No one helped him solve the problem.
   He solved _____. (by)

5. Unemployment is going down, or so the Government says.
   Unemployment _____. (according to)

6. Barbara's the only person I've told.
   I haven't _____. (except)

7. He didn't think before he spoke.
   He spoke _____. (without)

8. Is French the only foreign language she speaks?
   Does she speak _____. (besides)

9. Tom and a friend share a flat.
   Tom shares _____. (with)

10. Penny married Alec, although her parents disapproved.
    Penny married _____. (despite)

11. We can only accept a cheque if you have a cheque card.
    We can't _____. (without)

12. The only thing I haven't done is clean the bathroom.
    I've done _____. (apart from)

EXERCISE 6

Annie Moss writes an advice column in a magazine. Complete the following letters by choosing the appropriate verb, putting it in the correct form and combining it with the correct preposition from the boxes below. The first one has been done for you.

1

| talk   think   be interested |
| get bored |

| with   in   at   of   about |

Dear Annie,
My boyfriend (a) **is** only **interested in** football and he never (b) _____ _____ anything else. Quite honestly, I'm (c) _____ _____ his conversation. We were (d) _____ _____ getting married, but now I'm not so sure. What do you think?

Paula

2

| believe   worry   agree   shout |

| about   on   at   for   in |

Dear Annie,
I'm very (a) _____ _____ my son and his wife. They are always (b) _____ _____ each other and don't seem able to (c) _____ _____ anything. Personally, I don't (d) _____ _____ divorce, but they are obviously not happy together. Do you think I should say anything?

Betty

3

| suffer   think   ask   laugh |

| for   from   at   in   about |

Dear Annie,
  There's a girl in my office I find very attractive. In fact, I can't stop (a) _____ _____ her. The problem is, I (b) _____ extreme shyness. I would like to (c) _____ her _____ a date, but I'm afraid she might (d) _____ me. What do you think I should do?

Alan

4

| get tired   agree   look   complain |

| about   of   with   for   at |

Dear Annie,
  My boyfriend is very possessive. If I even (a) _____ another boy, he gets very angry. I'm (b) _____ _____ the situation, but if I (c) _____ his jealousy, he says I don't love him. I do love him, but I'm only seventeen and I want to enjoy myself. My mother thinks I should leave him. Do you (d) _____ her?

Liza

EXERCISE 7

Alice Withers is teaching a class of difficult ten-year-olds. Complete the following with suitable prepositions. Sometimes there is more than one correct answer. The first one has been done for you.

Late again, Jimmy, I see. The lesson started (1) **at** three o'clock, if you remember. Never mind. Sit over there (2) _____ Sandra, where I can see you. Now, what were we talking (3) _____? Ah yes, who was the king of England (4) _____ 1400? Doesn't anyone else know (5) _____ Patrick? Tracey, what are you reading (6) _____ your desk? No, it's no good trying to hide it (7) _____ your back. I'm not blind. Comics should be read (8) _____ the lesson, not (9) _____ it. Come and put it (10) _____ my desk, there's a good girl. Now, open your books (11) _____ page 24. Jimmy, what are you doing (12) _____ Sandra's book? Give it back to her at once. And don't look (13) _____ me like that. It's your own fault if you've come to school (14) _____ your books. Now, everyone, copy the picture (15) _____ page 24, and I want you all to have finished it (16) _____ the time the bell rings. Gary Browne, try and concentrate (17) _____ the lesson. You've been looking (18) _____ the window ever (19) _____ the class started. And don't think I can't see you just because you're sitting (20) _____ Thomas West. I think you'd better come and sit over here (21) _____ me. Are you chewing gum, Gary? You know that's (22) _____ the school rules. Go and throw it (23) _____ the waste-paper basket immediately! Now, I don't want to hear another word from anyone (24) _____ the bell rings. All right? Oh, dear, was that the bell? Right, you can all go home, (25) _____ David Peters. I want to speak to you, David, (26) _____ you leave.

EXERCISE 8

Complete the following news broadcast with the correct prepositions. The first one has been done for you.

Good evening, and here is the news.

The President of Romania arrived (1) **in** London this afternoon. He was met (2) _____ Victoria Station (3) _____ the Foreign Secretary. This is the first visit by a Romanian president (4) _____ more than twelve years. He will be staying (5) _____ the Romanian Consulate (6) _____ Friday.

The Prime Minister, who has been suffering (7) _____ a heavy cold, returned to work today. She said she felt much better, apart (8) _____ a bad cough. She is to meet the American Secretary of State (9) _____ Wednesday to talk (10) _____ future trade agreements (11) _____ the two countries.

Two jumbo jets narrowly missed each other when flying (12) _____ the Channel (13) _____ the weekend. The pilot of one aircraft said that he had to take emergency action when he saw the other aircraft coming (14) _____ him. Several passengers were later treated (15) _____ hospital (16) _____ shock.

The £2 a week pay increase for nurses has been severely criticised (17) _____ the Nurses' Union. Their spokesman, Tony Black, said, 'We had hoped (18) _____ a much bigger increase, but, as usual, we have been disappointed. Nurses' incomes are far (19) _____ the national average, and even (20) _____ this increase we still won't have enough to live (21) _____.'

Workmen pulling down a house (22) _____ Wellington Road, Cheshire, have found a number of valuable Roman objects (23) _____ the foundations. (24) _____ these objects were several coins, which, according (25) _____ the British Museum, are extremely rare.

A lioness escaped (26) _____ Manchester Zoo early this morning. She jumped (27) _____ her cage when her keeper opened the door to feed her. Residents living (28) _____ the zoo were asked to stay (29) _____ and to shut all doors and windows (30) _____ the lioness was recaptured.

And here is Bill Jones with the weather forecast.

Good evening. Well, I hope you've had a good day (31) _____ the weather! It's been very wet everywhere, and (32) _____ some areas it has rained continuously (33) _____ the day. However, the good news is that the rain should stop (34) _____ the night and (35) _____ the morning most of the clouds will have cleared away. Tomorrow will be a fine day, warm and sunny, with temperatures slightly (36) _____ average for the time of year, (37) _____ in coastal areas, where a cold wind (38) _____ the sea will keep temperatures down.

19 PHRASAL VERBS

BIRD'S EYE BOX: Phrasal verbs

House prices must **come down** again.	→	one particle (Exercises 1, 4 and 5)
I don't **get on with** him very well.	→	two particles (Exercises 1, 4 and 5)
She's got over **the shock**. Take off **your coat**/Take **your coat** off.	→	position of object (Exercise 2)
She's got over **it**. Take **it** off.	→	position of pronoun (Exercises 3, 4 and 5)

EXERCISE 1

Complete the following by putting a circle round the correct word or words in the brackets. When you need to use two words, you should number them (1 and 2) to show the correct word order.

Examples: If you hold (back /(on)/ off) a minute, sir, I'll try and connect you.

He's too far ahead. We'll never catch ((with)/ on /(up)) him now!
                                            2   1

1 When his car broke (in/out/down), he had to get the garage to repair it.
2 If you don't pay your phone bill, I'm afraid you'll be cut (off/up/out).
3 We're good friends now, but we didn't get (over/on/with) each other as children.
4 I see that Indian restaurant has closed (up/with/down). It didn't last long.
5 I'm terribly sorry I'm late. I ran (of/out/off) petrol on the way here.
6 Don't walk so fast! I can't keep (with/up/over) you!
7 I think I'd better set (of/up/off) a bit earlier tomorrow to miss the traffic.
8 Look at this letter from the bank manager! We've really got to cut (on/off/down) the amount we spend!
9 I had a terrible journey this morning. I was held (in/up/back) in the traffic for half an hour.
10 What time did you get (with/over/in) last night?

EXERCISE 2

Complete the following by choosing the appropriate phrasal verb and a suitable noun from the boxes below. If there are two possible positions for the noun, you should write both. Do not use any phrasal verb more than once.

Examples:

| put off | an idea |
| come up with | our holiday |

1. We were going away on Saturday, but we've had to
    (a) **put our holiday off**
    (b) **put off our holiday** for a couple of weeks.

2. We didn't know what to do about the problem until Nick
    (a) **came up with an idea.**
    (b) _____.

carry on with	an excuse
fill in	his father-in-law
get on with	the lesson
look after	petrol
make up	the lights
run into	the baby
run out of	this form
turn off	an old friend

1. John likes his wife's mother, but he doesn't
    (a) _____.
    (b) _____.

2. It's very kind of you to (a) _____ while I'm
    (b) _____
    out. I'm sure she won't be any trouble.

3. I really don't want to go to Ann's party. I'll have to
    (a) _____.
    (b) _____.

4. We'd better stop at a garage soon. We don't want to
    (a) _____.
    (b) _____.

5   Right, sir. If you'd like to join the club, could you
    (a) _____?
    (b) _____?

6   Sorry to interrupt. This won't take long, and then you can
    (a) _____.
    (b) _____.

EXERCISE 3

Complete the following by writing the correct alternative (a or b) in the box. The first one has been done for you.

1   I used to smoke, but I _____ a few years ago
    (a) gave it up   (b) gave up it | a |

2   I've had a terrible cold, but fortunately I've nearly _____.
    (a) got it over   (b) got over it | □ |

3   John's like his father, but Sheila _____.
    (a) takes me after   (b) takes after me | □ |

4   What time shall I _____?
    (a) pick you up   (b) pick up you | □ |

5   If you don't know what it means, _____ in the dictionary.
    (a) look it up   (b) look up it | □ |

6   I rather like these trousers. Can I _____?
    (a) try them on   (b) try on them | □ |

7   Look at this old diary. I _____ in a second-hand bookshop.
    (a) came it across   (b) came across it | □ |

8   They offered me the job, but the money was so bad I _____.
    (a) turned it down   (b) turned down it | □ |

9   Oh, you haven't lost your car keys again, have you? Well, this time I'm not helping you _____.
    (a) look them for   (b) look for them | □ |

10 My father's in favour of capital punishment, but I _____.
    (a) am it against   (b) am against it | □ |

EXERCISE 4

Complete the following with a pronoun and the correct particle or particles from the box below. Pay careful attention to the position of the pronoun.

back down forward of off on out to up with

Example: I wish I hadn't worn this thick sweater!
  Well, take **it off**, then.

1 'Your television programme begins in a minute, dear.'
  'Oh, could you turn _____ for me, please?'

2 'You're going on holiday next week, aren't you?'
  'Yes, we're going to Turkey. I'm really looking _____.'

3 'All they ever talk about on television nowadays is the general election!'
  'I know. I'm getting fed _____!'

4 'Is Tom flying to Canada on Saturday?'
  'Yes. We're going to the airport to see _____.'

5 'Have you finished what you were doing?'
  'No, but I can carry _____ later.'

6 'How much do I owe you?'
  'I'm not sure. I haven't worked _____ yet.'

7 'Mummy! Look what I've got!'
  'That's Barry's comic, not yours. Give _____ to him at once!'

8 'Don't you want to go on holiday with Brenda now?'
  'Not really, but I don't know how to get _____.'

9 'Can't we do something about the noise from the road-works?'
  'No, we can't. We'll just have to put _____.'

10 'Awful weather, isn't it?'
  'Yes, it's so depressing. It really gets _____.'

EXERCISE 5

Think of your own ideas to answer the following questions, using one of the phrasal verbs from the box below. Pay careful attention to any pronouns you may use. The first one has been done for you.

> get in get on with get over give back give up hold up look for
> look up make up take off try on turn off

1 'Do you smoke?'
   'Not any more. I've given it up.'

2 'Were you late again this morning?'
   '_____'

3 'What do you think of the new secretary?'
   '_____'

4 'How's your cold?'
   '_____'

5 'Have you still got that book I lent you?'
   '_____'

6 'Do you know Patricia's phone number?'
   '_____'

7 'Can I help you?'
   '_____'

8 'It's awfully hot in here, isn't it?'
   '_____'

20 LINKING WORDS

BIRD'S EYE BOX: Linking words

It's bright **and** sunny **but** the wind's cold.	→	relationships (Exercises 1 and 9)
He left **before** the match finished.	→	time (Exercises 2 and 9)
I'll tell him **when I see him**.	→	future time, present tense (Exercises 3 and 9)
She's upset **because** he shouted at her.	→	reason (Exercises 4 and 9)
The children behaved **so** badly **(that)** their mother sent them to bed.	→	result (Exercises 5 and 9)
He got the job, **although** he wasn't qualified.	→	contrast (Exercises 6 and 9)
He went to the manager **to** ask for a pay rise.	→	purpose (Exercises 7 and 9)
It's not **as** easy **as** you think!	→	comparison (Exercises 8 and 9)

EXERCISE 1

Using **and, but, either/or, neither/nor**, join each of the following groups of two or three sentences to form one sentence. Then complete the advertisement below. The first one has been done for you.

1. It's warm. It's sunny.
2. The beaches are empty. The sea is clear blue.
3. It's not crowded. It's not commercialized.
4. Life is quiet. There's plenty to do.
5. You can rent an apartment. You can stay in a two-star hotel.
6. The accommodation isn't luxurious. It's clean. It's comfortable.
7. Phone 01 762 9292. Call into our offices.

Are you looking for a quiet, relaxing holiday away from the crowds? Are you interested in an island where (1) **it's warm and sunny** all the year round? Then come to Mandrake Island where (2) _____!
(3) _____ on Mandrake Island. (4) _____ for those who want to get away from it all!

A two-week holiday costs from £250 per person. (5) _____. (6) _____ Interested?

For more details you can (7) _____.

EXERCISE 2

Complete the extract from a letter of application by using the linking words in the box to join the following notes. There is often more than one possible answer, but you should use each word or phrase once only. The first one has been done for you.

after as soon as before since until when while

1 Left school in 1976. Went to Italy for six months.
2 Returned to England. Then applied for three-year architectural course.
3 Studying at Manchester University. Developed an interest in photography.
4 Left the university in April 1980. Didn't take final exams in June.
5 Worked for advertising agency. Saved enough money.
6 Qualified. Have been employed by the *Daily News*.
7 Contract finishes in April. Shall be immediately available to start a new job.

(1) **After leaving school in 1976, I went to Italy for six months** to study architecture. (2) _____ at Manchester University. (3) _____, and so (4) _____.

I came to London and (5) _____

_____ to start a two-year diploma course in photography at Hampden College of Fine Arts, which I completed in 1983. (6) _____ as a sports photographer. However, (7) _____ _____.

EXERCISE 3

Expand the notes in the brackets to complete the second part of the following short dialogues.

Example: 'I'd like a word with you, Mary.'
        'OK. **I'll see you when the lesson finishes**.'
        (I/see/you when/the lesson/finish)

1. 'I hope I won't be too long.'
   'Don't hurry. _____.'
   (I/look/after the children/until/you/get/back)

2. 'Don't be too late, dear.'
   'No, I won't. _____.'
   (As soon as/the programme/end/I/come/to bed)

3. 'I'm afraid Tom's out. Can I take a message?'
   'Well, _____?'
   (you/ask/him to phone me/when/he/come/in?)

4. 'I hate flying! I'm always airsick!'
   'Never mind. _____.'
   (Once/the plane/land/you/feel/much better.)

5. 'You might need to put some more oil in the car, Derek.'
   'Don't worry. _____.'
   (I/check/it/before/I/go/out)

6. 'I've just got to cash a cheque.'
   'OK. _____.'
   (I/wait/in the car/while/you/be/in the bank?)

EXERCISE 4

Join the following ideas by choosing one of the linking words or phrases in the box below. Do not change the order of the sentences. There is often more than one possible answer, but you should use each word or phrase once only.

> as   because   because of   since   that's why   that's the reason why

Example: He was offered a better job. He left.
He was offered a better job. That's why he left.

1 I couldn't phone you last night. I left your number at work.
2 The flight was delayed. There was snow on the runway.
3 The train was cancelled. I was late.
4 He failed his driving test. He didn't stop at the red lights.
5 I'd better meet him at the station. He doesn't know the way.
6 It was far too expensive. I didn't buy it.

EXERCISE 5

Use the words in brackets to link together the following notes. (Sometimes you may still need to have two separate sentences.) Then complete the letter of complaint below. The first one has been done for you.

1 Men did a lot of damage. Will now have to replace table and two chairs. (such . . . that)

2 China and glass packed badly. A number of valuable pieces were broken. (so . . . that)

3 Men refused to carry any heavy furniture upstairs. Had to carry it myself. (so . . . that)

4 Injured my back. Have had to take a week off work. (as a result, consequently)

5 Should receive some compensation for damage and inconvenience. Have written to my solicitor. (therefore)

Dear Sir,

      Ref: Removal of furniture to 8 Windermere Road

I am writing to complain about the service provided by your removal company when I moved house last Wednesday.

In the first place, (1) **the men did such a lot of damage that I will now have to replace a table and two chairs.**

Secondly, (2) _____

_____

In addition, (3) _____

_____. (4) _____

and _____.

I am extremely dissatisfied with your company and feel strongly that (5) _____. _____

_____ who will contact you within the next few days.

Yours faithfully,

T. Booth

EXERCISE 6

Complete the following dialogue by choosing the appropriate word or phrase from the box below. Use each once only. The first one has been done for you.

| whereas   while   however   even though   on the other hand |
| but   although |

INTERVIEWER: What do you think Spicer's chances are of winning the championship? After all, he's only fourteen.

COACH: Well, I think his chances are very good, (1) **even though** he's so young. He's an extremely promising player.

INTERVIEWER: (2) _____ he doesn't have much experience, does he?

COACH: That's true. (3) _____ he's extremely enthusiastic and has lots of energy, which is very important.

— 131 —

INTERVIEWER: What about strength? Aren't the older players much stronger than he is?

COACH: Well, I was a little worried about that at first. (4) _____, it doesn't seem to make a great deal of difference. You see, (5) _____ other players have strength, Spicer has speed. He's extremely fast on his feet and extremely accurate too.

INTERVIEWER: So you think he's definitely a name to watch?

COACH: Oh, certainly. I'm confident that he'll do very well, (6) _____ he may not win the title this year.

EXERCISE 7

Use the words in brackets to link together the ideas in the following pairs of sentences. You will have to think of a suitable verb to complete the second part of the sentence. (There is sometimes more than one acceptable answer.)

Example: He hated arguments. So he kept his opinions to himself. (in order not to) **He kept his opinions to himself in order not to start an argument.**

1 She'd booked a holiday in America. So she had to get a visa. (to)

2 I don't want her card to arrive late. So I'll post it early. (so that)

3 He was away from his family a lot. So he gave up his career in the navy. (in order to)

4 His flatmate was asleep. So he turned his radio down. (so as not to)

5 They thought their children might not have a very good future in Britain. So they decided to emigrate to Australia. (in order that)

6 She didn't have many friends. So she joined a club. (so as to)

EXERCISE 8

Adam Waring writes a good food guide in a monthly magazine. Use the notes he made on his first and second visit to Vicino's restaurant to complete the article below. Use **as ... as** *or* **not as ... as** *in your answers. The first one has been done for you.*

First visit

1. Menu: choice of 8 dishes
2. Food: very well cooked
3. Service: efficient
4.   waiters friendly
5. Atmosphere: relaxed
6. Prices: £20–£30 per person
7. General impression: very good

Second visit

1. Menu: choice of 8 dishes
2. Food: quite well cooked
3. Service: efficient
4.   waiters friendly
5. Atmosphere: less relaxed
6. Prices: £15–£25 per person
7. General impression: quite good

Eat with Adam

This week I paid a second visit to Vicino's in Soho. Since I last ate there, the management has changed, so I was interested to see what it was like. There was still (1) **as much** choice on the menu **as** before, but the food was (2) _____ the last time I ate there. The service was just (3) _____ _____ previously, and the waiters were still (4) _____ _____ I remembered them. However, the atmosphere, though pleasant, was (5) _____ on my first visit. On the other hand, the prices were (6) _____ before. Generally, I was a little disappointed as it was (7) _____ I expected.

EXERCISE 9

Below is an extract from a chairman's speech to the Board of Directors. Complete each of the spaces with a suitable linking word. Where there is more than one possibility, try to use as many different words as possible. The first one has been done for you.

As you all know, we have been through an economic crisis recently and, (1) **as a result**, we have not made (2) _____ much profit _____ we did last year. The figures for this year are £2.5 million, (3) _____ last year our profits came to more than £6 million. (4) _____, we have had to reduce the workforce in some areas, and (5) _____ we decided,

reluctantly, to close down the Bromsgrove factory
(6) _____ it had been making a loss for some time.
  (7) _____ there is some good news.
(8) _____ increase sales in the Far East, we are, at present, negotiating a contract with Japan. These negotiations are in the early stages, (9) _____ I am confident that a contract will be signed. Obviously, I will let you know (10) _____ I have any definite news.

On a personal note, we are very sorry to say goodbye to one of our directors, Ernest Smith, who is taking early retirement (11) _____ ill health. He has been with the company (12) _____ it was formed in 1963. Brian Waite will be taking over as director, and I trust everyone will be (13) _____ co-operative _____ possible (14) _____ he can familiarise himself with the company. The date for our next board meeting still has to be fixed. It will (15) _____ be at the end of July (16) _____ the beginning of September, (17) _____ I have to visit Japan in August. You will be told (18) _____ the date is definite.

21 PUNCTUATION

BIRD'S EYE BOX: Punctuation

(M)y name's**(P)**edro and **(I)** come from**(M)**exico.	→	capital letters (Exercises 1, 2 and 5)
I've asked Jim**(,)** Pat and Dick**(,)** but not Sandra**(.)**	→	commas, full stops (Exercises 2 and 5)
Can I help you**(?)** Do be quiet**(!)**	→	question marks, exclamation marks (Exercises 3 and 5)
(")I**(')**ll be in the Teachers**(')** Room,**(")** she said.	→	quotation marks, apostrophes (Exercises 3 and 5)
Trivial**(:)** of small value**(;)** commonplace.	→	colon, semicolon (Exercises 4 and 5)
I hear Peter **(()** Mary's ex**(-)**husband**())** is getting married again **(—)** at least, Mary says so.	→	brackets, hyphens, dashes (Exercises 4 and 5)

EXERCISE 1

Correct the following by putting in capital letters where necessary.

1. i'm meeting brenda at victoria station on saturday afternoon. we'll probably do some shopping in bond street before going to the theatre in shaftesbury avenue.

2. sir richard algrave has been appointed british ambassador to brazil. he is well qualified for the position, having studied south american history at oxford university, as well as being a fluent portuguese speaker. he is due to take up the appointment after christmas.

3. what does scotland have to offer the tourist, besides the loch ness monster? well, how about a climb in the grampian mountains or a boat trip across to the isle of skye? interested? we're offering cut-price holidays in september. for more details contact highland tours, 136 regent street, london w 4.

EXERCISE 2

Punctuate the following by putting in commas and full stops where necessary. Remember you will need to put a capital letter at the beginning of a new sentence.

1. Unfortunately Prof Maurice Spitz is unable to give tonight's lecture however we are very pleased to welcome Dr Edmund Johnston instead Dr Johnston as many of you will know is an expert in Middle Eastern affairs

2. Certain foods e g eggs milk cheese butter etc are unhealthy if eaten in large quantities on the other hand bread and potatoes traditionally considered fattening are very important in a healthy diet

3.
> ## West Worth Co Ltd
>
> The company's annual dinner and dance will be held at the Queen's Hotel Wallace Rd Epsom on Sat Dec 5th at 800 p m

EXERCISE 3

Punctuate the following by putting in the necessary quotation marks, apostrophes, question marks and exclamation marks.

1. The man walked into the bank and pulled out a gun.
   Hands up he shouted. Dont move
   What do you want the bank manager asked, knowing very well what the answer would be.
   What do you think replied the man coldly. Now give me the keys to the safe

2. Help
   What was that asked Toby.
   I didnt hear anything, his friend Gerry replied.
   I thought I heard someone call help. It sounded like a womans voice.
   Listen There it is again Come on, lets see whats wrong

3. Ray and Eddy watched in astonishment as Paul stopped the Porsche outside Eddys house.
   What a fantastic car said Ray.
   Where did you get it asked Eddy.
   Paul enjoyed seeing the look of astonishment on his friends faces.
   Its my brothers car, he said. Hes lent it to me while hes away.
   You lucky thing said Ray. Can we have a go

EXERCISE 4

Below is the introduction to a book on vegetable growing. Make the extract clearer by adding brackets, dashes, hyphens, colons and semicolons where you think appropriate.

Vegetables are for everyone not just vegetarians! And yet we, the British, eat fewer vegetables annually eighty five kilos per person than most other Europeans. However, this may all change now that more people are becoming interested in growing their own.

Home grown vegetables have three definite advantages over shop bought ones you can choose the kinds of vegetables you wish to grow you can pick and eat them the moment they are ready you can save money not to mention the satisfaction of having grown them yourself!

In this book we have included thirty five different types of vegetables. Some are old favourites carrots, lettuces, potatoes while others are less well known. And, in addition, we have included a special section on growing herbs pages 116–19.

Which vegetables you choose to grow the old favourites or something new is entirely up to you.

EXERCISE 5

Punctuate the following letter and newspaper article correctly.

1

dear bill

congratulations i hear youve been promoted to managing director how about meeting for lunch to celebrate well be away for a week in mid aug the annual visit to my mother in laws home in ireland but well be back on the twenty fourth why dont you give me a ring so we can arrange something

regards

terry

p s dont know if youve got my new number its 743 9631 ext 41

residents of banbury road ipswich are angry about yesterdays decision by the local council to allow the sunday market in banbury road to continue the residents have three main complaints the excessive noise from 700 a m every sunday the increase in traffic which endangers childrens lives one child was knocked down last month the amount of litter in the street after the market closes

mrs hilda west who has lived in the road for more than twenty five years said im furious its all right for the councillors they dont have to live here this used to be a quiet road before the market arrived

the residents now plan to write to their local m p william davis the council refused to comment on their decision

ANSWERS TO THE EXERCISES

(Answers given in brackets are acceptable but not as likely.)

1 Nouns

EXERCISE 1

2	secretaries	6	lady	10	keys	14	photographs
3	person	7	teeth	11	children	15	bush
4	shoe	8	policemen	12	box	16	foot
5	fish/(fishes)	9	knife	13	tomatoes		

EXERCISE 2

2	headlines	5	earrings	8	armchair
3	housework	6	newspaper	9	handbag
4	ashtray	7	toothbrush	10	notebook

EXERCISE 3

1	information	3	scales	5	pyjamas	7	advice
2	glasses	4	homework	6	furniture	8	scissors

EXERCISE 4

2 c 3 b 4 a 5 b 6 c 7 a 8 b

2 Articles

EXERCISE 1

the must be used in the following:
1 a, b, c   3 a, b, c, d   5 a, b   7 a, b, c, d, e
2 a, b, c   4 c   6 a, f, g 8 b

EXERCISE 2

the must be used in 1, 6, 7, 8, 13, 18, 19, 20; it may be omitted in 11

EXERCISE 3

1 a (sometimes people still say 'an (h)otel')
2 an   4 a   6 a   8 a
3 an   5 an 7 an

EXERCISE 4

2 three times a week
3 four times a year
4 twice a month
5 once a day
6 three times a year

EXERCISE 5

2 35p a
3 £1.58 a
4 23p a pint
5 49p a litre
6 30p a can
7 £2.22 a kilo
8 £3.00 a litre

EXERCISE 6

1 a
2 –
3 an
4 a
5 –
6 –
7 a
8 an
9 –
10 an

EXERCISE 7

1	the	10	the	19	The	28	an
2	The	11	A	20	A	29	a
3	–	12	the	21	–	30	The
4	the	13	–	22	a	31	the
5	The	14	the	23	the	32	–
6	the	15	A	24	A	33	the
7	The	16	a	25	the	34	An
8	a	17	an	26	the	35	the
9	a	18	the	27	–	36	the

3 Pronouns

EXERCISE 1

1	us	6	her	11	him	16	him	21	yours
2	me	7	her	12	my	17	her	22	yours
3	their	8	her	13	yours	18	his		
4	them	9	his	14	you	19	hers		
5	your	10	him	15	ours	20	mine		

EXERCISE 2

2 those
3 that
4 these
5 this
6 these
7 those
8 that

EXERCISE 3

2 himself
3 –
4 ourselves
5 yourself
6 –
7 yourselves
8 themselves

EXERCISE 4

1 each other/one another
2 each other/one another
3 themselves
4 yourself
5 ourselves
6 each other/one another
7 each other (one another)
8 themselves
9 each other (one another)
10 each other (one another)
11 each other (one another)
12 yourself

EXERCISE 5

1 who
2 whose
3 which
4 whom
5 whom
6 whose
7 who
8 which

EXERCISE 6

1 That's the Smith family, who had the room next to ours.
2 That's Señor Bueno, whose daughter worked in the hotel.
3 That's the Tropicana Disco, (which) we went to a couple of times.
4 That's the local bookshop, which sold English newspapers.
5 That's the Pablo family we met on the beach.
6 That's Señora Pablo, whose brother works in London.
7 That's Roberto, the waiter, who showed us how to dance flamenco.
8 That's the hotel cat, which used to follow us to the beach.

EXERCISE 7

1 Heavy snow, which fell unexpectedly during the night, has blocked most roads in the north of Scotland.
2 Cardinal Onzo of Brazil, with whom the Archbishop of Canterbury had talks/who (whom) the Archbishop of Canterbury had talks with earlier this week, left from Heathrow this morning.
3 Amateur radio enthusiast Paul Little, who heard the SOS signal on his transmitter, saved the lives of nine Spanish seamen last night.
4 Simon Walsh, twenty-two, whose father is the Conservative M.P. for Lower Trauton, appeared at Manchester Crown Court today, charged with driving without a licence.
5 A priceless seventeenth-century painting, which was stolen over twenty-five years ago, has been discovered in a house in Berkshire.
6 Mr and Mrs Andrew Baker, whose house was demolished by mistake, have received more than £200,000 compensation from their local council.
7 The famous 1920s beauty Nancy Loughborough, for whom the well-known song 'Beautiful' was written/who (whom) the well-known song 'Beautiful' was written for, has died in her sleep at eighty-two.
8 And finally, Mrs Brenda Tyler, who lost more than thirty-five kilos in six months, has been nominated Slimmer of the Year.

EXERCISE 8

1 someone/body else
2 anyone/body
3 nothing else
4 everyone/body else
5 anything else
6 everything
7 anyone/body else
8 something
9 no one/nobody else
10 nothing
11 something else
12 someone/body

EXERCISE 9

1	your	5	anyone else	9	each other	13	something
2	this	6	him	10	those	14	us
3	us	7	whose	11	yourself	15	myself
4	who	8	everyone	12	our	16	everyone else

4 Question Words

EXERCISE 1

1	When	3	Which	5	Whose	7	How often	9	Who
2	Why	4	How	6	Where	8	What	10	How far

EXERCISE 2

2 Where did the Cluan family live?
3 Why was Cluan in serious financial trouble?
4 When/What time did he return?
5 What did the nurse hear?
6 How did he kill her?
7 Who did he intend to murder?
8 Why did he make a mistake?
9 Where did he drive to?
10 What did they find inside his car?

EXERCISE 3

1	Who else	3	where else	5	Why else
2	What else	4	How else	6	When else

EXERCISE 4

2 Which/What university did you go to?
3 What qualifications have you got/do you have?
4 Which/What languages do you speak?
5 Which/What countries have you worked in?
6 Which/What sports are you interested in?

EXERCISE 5

2 How often do the trains go/leave/run?
3 When/What time does it leave?
4 Which is the best train/one (to catch)?
5 How long does it take?
6 How much is the fare/a return ticket?/How much does it cost?
7 Where shall I meet you?/Where shall we meet?
8 Whose car (are you borrowing)?
9 Who's Peter?
10 What (sort/type/make of) car is it/has he got?
11 What clothes shall I bring?/What shall I bring to wear?
12 What are we going to do? Where are we going?

EXERCISE 6

1 How	3 What	5 What a	7 How	9 How
2 What a	4 How	6 How	8 What	10 What a

5 Adjectives

EXERCISE 1

2 the poor	5 the sick	8 the homeless
3 the wealthy	6 the old	9 the strong
4 the young	7 The unemployed	10 The weak

EXERCISE 2

1 That meal was really delicious.
2 The exam doesn't look terribly difficult.
3 It's a very embarrassing situation.
4 The children didn't seem very excited.
5 It's an extremely interesting programme.

EXERCISE 3

1 interesting, (the) most interesting
2 farther/further, (the) farthest/(the) furthest
3 bad, (the) worst
4 easier, (the) easiest
5 valuable, more valuable
6 thinner, (the) thinnest
7 old, elder/older
8 more aggressive, (the) most aggressive
9 wide, (the) widest
10 better, (the) best

EXERCISE 4

The Supercontinental

2 It's bigger/larger. It has more rooms.
3 It's dearer/more expensive.
4 It has more facilities.
5 It has a wider/bigger choice on the menu.
6 It's more efficient/less friendly/more impersonal.
7 It's noisier. It's less comfortable.

The Glencairn Hotel

1 It's farther from the city centre.
2 It's smaller. It has fewer rooms.
3 It's cheaper/less expensive.
4 It has fewer facilities.
5 It has a smaller choice on the menu. The food's better.
6 It's less efficient/slower/more friendly.
7 It's quieter. It's more comfortable.

EXERCISE 5

2 the longest
3 the most exhausting because the altitude made the air thin
4 the coldest because the wind was icy
5 the worst because the weather was appalling
6 the most frustrating because it was impossible to climb
7 the most depressing because he didn't make much progress
8 the hardest because the climb was very difficult
9 the most exciting because he reached the top (at last)

EXERCISE 6

1. the latest
2. the most impressive
3. smaller
4. more spacious
5. the most comfortable
6. the fastest
7. the most economical
8. more
9. better
10. more efficient
11. easier
12. the safest
13. (the) most reliable
14. the best

6 Adverbs

EXERCISE 1

(Suggested answers)

1. He's starting in two days' time/at the end of the month/in the morning/on Tuesday/this afternoon/today.
2. I haven't seen him since the end of the month/since Tuesday/since last week/this afternoon/today.
3. I'll pay you back in two days' time/at/by the end of the month/in/by the morning/on/by Tuesday/by this afternoon/by today/this afternoon/today.
4. It usually arrives at the end of the month/in the morning/on Tuesdays.
5. He should have done it in two days' time/at/by the end of the month/by the morning/on/by Tuesday/by this afternoon/by today/a month ago/last week.
6. She left at the end of the month/in the morning/on Tuesday/a month ago/last week/this afternoon/today.

EXERCISE 2

2 a	5 c (b is just possible)	8 b
3 c (b is also possible)	6 b, c	9 c
4 b	7 b, c	10 c

EXERCISE 3

2. occasionally/sometimes gets a part in the theatre
3. is frequently/often out of work
4. usually/generally helps in a friend's restaurant
5. is always/continually worried about money
6. sometimes/occasionally help him financially
7. rarely/hardly ever sees them
8. occasionally/sometimes gets depressed
9. would never/wouldn't ever consider doing anything else

EXERCISE 4

2. easily
3. hard/hardly
4. thoroughly
5. in an unfriendly way/manner
6. well
7. badly
8. angrily
9. disapprovingly/in a disapproving way/manner
10. fast

EXERCISE 5

(Suggested answers)

2 very/extremely
3 well/efficiently/thoroughly
4 well/efficiently/thoroughly
5 fast/accurately/quickly/well
6 fast/accurately/quickly/well
7 fluently/perfectly/well
8 quite/fairly/very/extremely
9 well
10 punctually/early
11 very/extremely
12 hard

EXERCISE 6

2 longer
3 more thoroughly
4 better
5 farther/further
6 more quickly/more efficiently

EXERCISE 7

(Suggested answers)

1 drive/walk/go faster/more quickly
2 work/study harder/more carefully
3 play more quietly/less noisily
4 drive more slowly/less fast/more carefully
5 played (even) worse
6 speak more loudly/more slowly/more clearly/less quickly

EXERCISE 8

1 (a) most carefully   (b) most sensibly
2 (a) the most efficiently   (b) the best   (c) the least
3 (a) most favourably   (b) the most enthusiastically
4 (a) the most   (b) the hardest
5 (a) most apologetically   (b) most unreasonably

EXERCISE 9

(Suggested answers)

2 extremely/very
3 never
4 best/fastest
5 well
6 regularly/daily
7 recently/lately
8 harder/longer/more
9 farther/longer
10 hardly
11 very/extremely/quite
12 very/extremely
13 very/extremely
14 close
15 Luckily/Fortunately
16 ever
17 seriously/badly/severely
18 successfully/safely

7 Quantifiers

EXERCISE 1

2	much	4	many	6	much	8	much
3	many	5	much	7	many		

EXERCISE 2

1 a great deal of/plenty of
2 A number of/Plenty of
3 plenty of
4 a number of
5 plenty
6 a great deal of

EXERCISE 3

2 a lot of/lots of/plenty of/a number of
3 many/(a lot)
4 a lot of/lots of/a number of/many
5 much/a great deal of/a lot of
6 many
7 a lot of/lots of/a number of
8 much/a great deal of/a lot of
9 many
10 a number
11 a number of/a lot of/lots of
12 plenty of/a lot of/lots of

EXERCISE 4

2	a little	4	a few	6	a few	8	a little
3	a little	5	a little	7	a few		

EXERCISE 5

1 (b) a few   (c) a little
2 (a) few   (b) little   (c) few
3 (a) a few (b) little   (c) a few   (d) a little

EXERCISE 6

2 fewer
3 less acceleration
4 less petrol
5 fewer gears
6 less choice of colour
7 fewer extras

EXERCISE 7

2 (a) any   (b) some   5 any
3 (a) some   (b) some   (c) any   6 (a) any   (b) some
4 some

EXERCISE 8

2 a little
3 few
4 several/quite a few/a few
5 any
6 several/quite a few/a few
7 little
8 fewer
9 some/quite a few
10 less
11 any
12 several/quite a few/a few
13 several/a few/some
14 any

8 Modals

EXERCISE 1

2 Could I have the salt
3 I'll have a look at it
4 Shall we go to the cinema
5 Will you stay for lunch?
6 will/could you get some stamps
7 Will you have another piece?
8 Shall I show you how to use it?
9 Shall we eat out
10 I'll get them

EXERCISE 2

(Suggested answers)

1 (b) would (I'd) sooner stay
2 (a) would (he'd) like (to have)   (b) would he rather have
   (c) would (he'd) prefer to choose/buy
3 (a) would you rather go   (b) would (I'd) sooner not go
4 (a) Would you prefer to eat at home/stay in   (b) would (I'd) sooner go out/eat out
   (c) would (I'd) like to have
5 (a) I wouldn't like to have/do   (b) would (I'd) rather have/earn
6 (a) would (I'd) prefer not to make   (b) would (I'd) like to have

EXERCISE 3

1 had (We'd) better
2 had (You'd) better not
3 should/ought to
4 Hadn't you better
5 Should/Ought violent films to
6 shouldn't/ought not to
7 had (We'd) better not
8 had (I'd) better
9 Hadn't you better
10 shouldn't/ought not to

EXERCISE 4

2 Can we leave
3 could/may/might turn
4 Could/May/Can I use
5 may/might not have
6 could always come
7 can't read
8 couldn't take

EXERCISE 5

1 (b) can't   (c) could/was able to   (d) might/could
   (e) can/will be able to/will be allowed to

2 (a) was not allowed to/couldn't (b) can't (c) couldn't/wasn't able to
  (d) may/might not (e) will be able to/can (f) could/might/may
3 (a) could/may/might (b) aren't allowed to/can't
  (c) can't/aren't allowed to (d) won't be able to/can't
  (e) weren't allowed to (f) might/may

EXERCISE 6

(The answers in brackets are possible but not as good.)

1 a   2 a/b   3 b (a)   4 b (a)   5 a/b   6 a   7 a   8 b

EXERCISE 7

2 mustn't get up yet
3 needn't/don't have to say it again
4 needn't/don't have to tell the others
5 mustn't eat it
6 mustn't say it again
7 needn't/don't have to drive so fast
8 needn't/don't have to get up yet
9 mustn't do it
10 needn't/don't have to eat/do it
11 mustn't drive so fast
12 needn't/don't have to do/eat it

EXERCISE 8

1 (b) must be
2 (a) must know   (b) must have seen
3 (a) can't be   (b) can't have gone   (c) must be
4 (a) can't have climbed   (b) must have (had)
5 (a) can't be   (b) must have put
6 (a) must be   (b) can't have lost   (c) must have

EXERCISE 9

2 Neighbours used to call in on each other.
3 People used to leave their doors open.
4 There didn't use to be so much crime.
5 The traffic didn't use to be as bad.
6 Children used to play in the street.
7 Most mothers didn't use to go out to work/used to stay at home.
8 Mothers used to stay at home.

EXERCISE 10

(The students have been asked to use **would** whenever possible; **used to** can be used in every case and is not incorrect, though **would** is preferred in 1, 3, 4, 6 and 8.)

1 would (used to)   3 would (used to)
2 used to   4 would (used to)

5	used to	7	used to
6	would (used to)	8	would (used to)

EXERCISE 11

(Suggested answers)

2 Shall
3 I'd rather/sooner/prefer to/I'll
4 you'd better not/shouldn't/mustn't
5 won't be able to
6 can't
7 used to
8 must
9 might
10 should/ought to
11 Would you like to
12 I'd rather/sooner/prefer to
13 We'd better/should/ought to/must
14 needn't/don't have to
15 Can/Could/May/Shall
16 Can
17 shall
18 I'll
19 could
20 could/were able to

9 Tenses

Although verb + not is always correct, it is not normally used in informal writing.

EXERCISE 1

2	was	9	does	16	has	23	don't
3	didn't	10	doesn't	17	Have	24	did
4	was	11	were	18	had	25	doesn't
5	had	12	was	19	didn't	26	doesn't
6	are	13	didn't	20	is	27	have
7	is	14	hasn't	21	am	28	don't
8	are	15	Do	22	have	29	be

EXERCISE 2

1 (b) think   (c) am (I'm) doing   (d) are (you're) pressing   (e) enlarges
   (f) need   (g) is (It's) working

2 (a) see   (b) is going   (c) know   (d) am (I'm) seriously considering
   (e) don't often use   (f) does your wife think   (g) agrees   (h) doesn't like

3 (a) is (he's) seeing   (b) Is he expecting   (c) have   (d) are (we're) running
   (e) don't expect   (f) don't mind

4 (a) are we waiting   (b) expect   (c) is (he's) having   (d) is (car's) always
   going   (e) am (I'm) not waiting   (f) don't want   (g) Are you coming

5 (a) are you making   (b) smells   (c) am (I'm) trying   (d) sounds
   (e) cut   (f) just add   (g) makes   (h) tastes   (i) doesn't look

6 (a) do you think   (b) find   (c) is (She's) always making   (d) never listens
   (e) know   (f) mean   (g) feel   (h) think   (i) is (she's) trying
   (j) only succeeds/is (she's) only succeeding

EXERCISE 3

2 Let's go for a walk.
3 don't forget your key
4 Do tell me about it!
5 Do not disturb.
6 Turn off the electricity supply
7 say I'm out
8 Let's go somewhere else

EXERCISE 4

(Suggested answers)

1 They were driving home when the trouble started/when they began arguing/when it started to rain.
2 He didn't know what to do when the trouble started/when they began arguing/when he left school/when the car broke down.
3 He's been working here while/since you've been away/since he left school.
4 I haven't seen him since the trouble started/while/since you've been away/since he left school.
5 We'd already left when/before/by the time the trouble started/when/before they began arguing/when/before it started to rain.
6 The police arrived when/as soon as/just as the trouble started/when/just as they began arguing/when/while/just as he was counting the money.
7 She was keeping watch when the trouble started/when they began arguing/when/ while he was counting the money.
8 We'd been enjoying ourselves before the trouble started/before they began arguing/ before the car broke down/before it started to rain.

EXERCISE 5

2 happened
3 was
4 had lost/had been losing
5 was watching
6 noticed
7 was she doing/did she do
8 seemed
9 kept
10 wanted
11 was watching
12 Had you ever seen
13 wasn't
14 picked
15 put
16 didn't pay
17 left
18 did you do
19 followed
20 asked
21 emptied/had emptied
22 found
23 had taken
24 hadn't paid
25 have you worked/been working
26 have you caught
27 have (I've) learnt

EXERCISE 6

(The answers in brackets are also possible but less probable.)

1 a (b)   4 c (a)   7 a (b)   10 c
2 d (b, a) 5 c (a)   8 d (b)
3 a   6 d (a)   9 a (c)

EXERCISE 7

2 they'll be driving to Dover
3 they'll have arrived in Dover
4 they'll have crossed the Channel/ arrived in Calais.

5 they'll be having lunch in Calais
6 they'll be driving to Bruges
7 they'll have got to Bruges
8 they'll have reached Brussels
9 they'll have been travelling

EXERCISE 8

2 have (I've) been meaning
3 haven't had
4 know
5 started
6 have (I've) been working
7 like
8 don't finish
9 get
10 will (I'll) tell
11 am (I'm) going to take/am (I'm) taking
12 am (I'm) thinking/was thinking
13 has invited
14 is going
15 Have you made
16 let's meet
17 saw
18 have
19 will (I'll) phone
20 Give

EXERCISE 9

1 (b) was taking (c) jumped (d) pulled (e) was playing/had been playing (f) happened

2 (a) have protested/are protesting (b) drive/have been driving (c) complained (d) make (e) haven't been able (f) are (they're) always breaking (g) will be (h) doesn't stop

3 (a) will be collecting/are collecting (b) hope (c) will have raised (d) said (e) need (f) will help (g) are looking

4 (a) think (b) started (c) burnt (d) called (e) arrived (f) had fallen (g) are now demolishing

5 (a) has died (b) had lived/had been living (c) taught/had taught (d) retired (e) will take

6 (a) will open/is to open (b) has written (c) will be signing/will sign

EXERCISE 10

2 found
3 had been dripping
4 was
5 saw
6 called
7 answered
8 went
9 hasn't come
10 will (I'll) tell
11 comes
12 don't expect
13 will (he'll) be
14 hung
15 sat
16 rang
17 believe
18 called
19 have you been
20 demanded
21 have (I've) been waiting
22 have you been doing
23 answered
24 had
25 was driving
26 have (I've) only just got
27 haven't even had
28 is getting
29 said
30 are you going to repair
31 Don't worry
32 replied
33 will (I'll) have
34 will (I'll) come
35 put
36 went
37 was still dripping
38 had (he'd) put
39 emptied
40 sat
41 picked
42 was dialling
43 rang
44 said
45 think
46 will (I'll) have

10 Unreal Past

EXERCISE 1

2 you grew up
3 (high) time you did some work
4 It's (high) time you earned some money.
5 It's (high) time you found a job.
6 It's (high) time you started to consider your father and me.

EXERCISE 2

2 I'd rather/sooner you didn't say anything to anyone
3 I'd rather/sooner you thought about it carefully
4 I'd rather/sooner you were honest and told me
5 I'd rather/sooner you did what you thought was right
6 I'd rather/sooner you didn't phone me at work

EXERCISE 3

2 I wish/If only I weren't (wasn't) so shy.
3 I wish/If only I hadn't come to the party.
4 I wish/If only I didn't feel nervous.
5 I wish/If only I'd (I had) stayed at home.
6 I wish/If only I hadn't put on a suit.
7 I wish/If only I had more self-confidence.
8 I wish/If only I could dance.

EXERCISE 4

2 suppose you knew who he was
3 suppose he were (was) a friend of yours
4 suppose you'd been in the area
5 Suppose you'd (you had) heard or seen something suspicious
6 suppose you had some information and could help the police
7 suppose he'd (he had) attacked

EXERCISE 5

(Suggested answers)

2 as if/as though he ran the company
3 as if/as though I were (was) a complete idiot
4 as if/as though she'd (she had) won a fortune
5 as if/as though I'd (I had) said something terrible
6 as if/as though she lived in a palace
7 as if/as though I'd (I had) committed a crime

11 To + Infinitive/Infinitive without To

EXERCISE 1

(Suggested answers)

2	to catch/get/meet	4	to do	6	to buy/rent/share	8	to think
3	to see	5	to wear	7	to say		

EXERCISE 2

2	to employ	3	to have	4	to say	5	to work	6	to let	7	to give

EXERCISE 3

2 stupid to say that young people are lazy
3 aren't old enough to have any experience
4 are unwilling to offer them jobs
5 are quick to learn
6 are keen to work hard
7 very sad to see young people out of work
8 will be too depressed to look for jobs

EXERCISE 4

2	how to change	4	where to go	6	whether to stay
3	who to ask	5	which to join	7	what to say

EXERCISE 5

(Suggested answers)

1 to find out/ask about/for
2 library to return/change/take her books back
3 Marino's/the restaurant to book/reserve a table for two (on Saturday)
4 to the Post Office to buy/get some stamps
5 the hairdresser's to make an appointment (for Friday afternoon)
6 to the bank to get (out)/withdraw/deposit £50
7 the dentist to cancel her appointment (at 10.30 on Tuesday)
8 Anne to invite/ask her to lunch on Sunday

EXERCISE 6

2	let you eat	4	makes you feel	6	let you have	8	let you know
3	make me laugh	5	make your legs ache	7	let me think		

EXERCISE 7

2 noticed Sherriff fall down
3 I didn't hear the referee blow his whistle
4 I saw Sherriff trip over
5 I didn't notice Foreman touch him
6 heard someone shout
7 felt someone push him from behind
8 I've watched Foreman play lots of matches
9 I've never seen him foul before

— 153 —

EXERCISE 8

2	to listen	9	do	16	to stay	23	worry
3	to talk	10	remember	17	(to) get	24	to accept
4	to go	11	hit	18	say	25	to do
5	know	12	to show	19	have	26	to meet
6	to say	13	do	20	to continue	27	expect
7	to give	14	to discuss	21	to return	28	to see
8	make	15	do	22	to do		

12 Gerund

EXERCISE 1

1 Looking after young children is very tiring.
2 Not getting the job depressed him.
3 Sharing a flat sometimes causes arguments.
4 Being a teacher/Teaching requires a lot of patience.
5 Never going out must be boring.
6 Not having any friends must make him lonely.

EXERCISE 2

2 Exporting more goods will help the economy.
3 Training more teachers will raise the level of education.
4 Providing more entertainment for young people will keep them out of trouble.
5 Cutting taxation will help the lower-paid workers.
6 Employing more policemen will make our streets safer.

EXERCISE 3

2	to leave	7	being	12	to be	17	telling
3	letting	8	to say	13	trying	18	to transfer
4	wondering	9	working	14	to work	19	to go
5	to leave	10	doing	15	staying	20	staying
6	working	11	telling	16	feeling		

EXERCISE 4

(Suggested answers)

2 robbing/attacking
3 stopping
4 hitting/knocking down
5 questioning/talking to/interviewing
6 starting a fight/speeding/drunken driving
7 leaving/going home
8 starting again/training for his next fight
9 travelling/touring/singing/performing
10 going on tour/travelling
11 losing
12 braking/accelerating/steering
13 flying on/travelling on
14 taking off/flying
15 landing at/returning to
16 being so kind/looking after her
17 spending
18 leaving/keeping
19 opening/looking in/taking the top off
20 causing the trouble/frightening everyone/being a nuisance

EXERCISE 5

1	a	3	b	5	b	7	a	9	b
2	b	4	a	6	a	8	b	10	a

EXERCISE 6

2	inviting	7	driving	12	to bring	17	hearing
3	to come	8	to catch	13	getting	18	to tell
4	driving	9	meeting	14	reading (to read)	19	to wait
5	to come	10	walking	15	to have	20	to let
6	sitting	11	sitting	16	seeing		

13 Participles

EXERCISE 1

1	Fallen	3	rising	5	missing	7	Worried
2	amazing	4	broken	6	Burst	8	exhausting

EXERCISE 2

2	interested	5	astonishing	8	embarrassing	11	confusing/
3	disappointed	6	impressed	9	surprised		(confused)
4	exciting	7	amusing	10	bored	12	disappointing

EXERCISE 3

1	arriving/waiting	3	left	5	bought
2	damaged	4	wearing	6	meeting

EXERCISE 4

(Suggested answers)

2 making
3 Looking/Peering/Staring
4 smoking
5 talking/speaking
6 laughing/smiling
7 reading/looking at
8 looking at/speaking to/taking any notice of
9 carrying
10 watching/looking at/staring at
11 Turning/Looking
12 Taking/Pulling

EXERCISE 5

1 Not acceptable. While I was driving along the road, a car pulled out in front of me.
2 Acceptable
3 Not acceptable. The police found a body hidden in the wood.
4 Not acceptable. The traffic slowed down and, looking left and right, she crossed the road.
5 Acceptable.
6 Not acceptable. While he was walking across the golf course, a golf ball hit him.

EXERCISE 6

2 looking at some girls sunbathing
3 see something moving
4 notice Dave windsurfing
5 see the shark coming
6 hear Rita shouting
7 feel the/your surfboard rocking
8 hear Dave/you screaming

EXERCISE 7

(Suggested answers)

1 I heard someone crying in the next room.
2 I felt a cold hand touch me.
3 I saw something floating in the air above my head.
4 I heard a door slam suddenly.
5 I saw a white face appear and then disappear.
6 I felt/saw something crawling up my arm.
7 I heard the wind howling outside.
8 I felt someone tap me on the shoulder.

EXERCISE 8

(Suggested answers)

2 having planned/finalised/thought out
3 having killed/shot/murdered
4 having disposed of/got rid of/buried
5 Having thrown away/disposed of/got rid of
6 Having made
7 Having taken/stolen/hidden
8 having committed

EXERCISE 9

2 Annoyed, demanding
3 travelling
4 broken, hidden
5 Realising, hoping
6 Having taken
7 swollen, surrounding
8 Lying, worried, depressed
9 wanting
10 having heard

14 The Passive

EXERCISE 1

2 were held up
3 Is the road being repaired?
4 had been warned
5 has the number been changed
6 was being used
7 are kept
8 was offered
9 is being/is going to be pulled down

EXERCISE 2

1. (b) was stolen   (c) has already been arrested
2. (a) were taken   (b) were sent   (c) was started
3. (a) has been banned   (b) was told   (c) had been stopped
4. (a) has been found   (b) is being looked
5. (a) was being loaded   (b) was treated/is being treated

EXERCISE 3

1. is being written by Adrian Holt, the well-known composer
2. was killed with a knife
3. mother of three has been arrested for shop-lifting
4. accident was almost certainly caused by ice on the road.
5. is being repaired
6. the food had been injected with poison

EXERCISE 4

2. Prescriptions should be collected before midday.
3. Shop-lifters will be arrested.
4. Tennis-rackets can be borrowed on request.
5. Reference books may not be taken out of the library.
6. These instructions must not be removed.

EXERCISE 5

2. what can be done
3. the problem could be solved
4. the public transport system has to be improved
5. fares ought to be reduced
6. more money should be provided by the Government
7. people would be encouraged to leave their cars at home
8. higher car-park charges need to be introduced
9. more traffic wardens ought to be employed
10. drivers would be discouraged
11. will anything be done about the problem
12. a solution must be found quickly

EXERCISE 6

2. To be taken after meals.
3. Not to be given to children under five.
4. To be used only with soft contact lenses.
5. Not to be sprayed near eyes or mouth.
6. Not to be used on broken or sensitive skin.

EXERCISE 7

2. are to be given   5. are to be returned
3. is to be taken over   6. is to be opened
4. are to be increased

EXERCISE 8

2 are kept/must be kept
3 was pushed
4 had been taken
5 had been tied/were tied
6 had been drugged/were/was drugged
7 was being watched
8 was unlocked
9 were kept/would be kept
10 are hidden/have been hidden
11 will be killed
12 was locked
13 was made
14 could not be broken
15 could not be opened
16 was trapped

15 Question Tags

EXERCISE 1

1 hasn't he
2 hadn't you
3 could I
4 aren't I
5 was it
6 won't you
7 haven't they
8 do they
9 wouldn't you

EXERCISE 2

2 wasn't it
3 did you
4 does it
5 can I
6 isn't it
7 aren't they
8 have you
9 should I
10 were you
11 do you
12 won't you

EXERCISE 3

The following combinations are all possible, provided that a positive sentence has a negative tag and a negative sentence has a positive tag.

| Patrick | must | have missed the train, | mustn't | he? |
| They | might | | mightn't | they? |

| Patrick | is | here, | isn't | he? |
| It | isn't | | is | it? |

Everyone's here, aren't they?

You	will	tell her,	won't	you?
They	won't		will	they?
Patrick	must		mustn't	he?
We	mustn't		must	we?

They	have	got the keys,	haven't	they?
We	haven't		have	we?
You				you?

| You | aren't | thinking, | are | you? |
| They | weren't | | were | they? |

It	will	be very nice,	won't	it?
	won't		will	
	might		mightn't	
	would		wouldn't	
	wouldn't		would	

You	will	come,	won't	you?
Patrick	might		mightn't	he?
They				they?
Everyone				

You	have	paid the bill,	haven't	you?
They	haven't		have	they?
We				we?

You	are	late,	aren't	you?
We	aren't		are	we?
	were		weren't	
	weren't		were	

Patrick is late, isn't he?

EXERCISE 4

2 wasn't it (a)   5 isn't it (b)   8 have you (c)
3 did you (c)   6 does he (a)   9 can't you (a)
4 don't you (b)   7 didn't I (b)   10 would you (c or b)

16 Conditionals

EXERCISE 1

1 wait, will (I'll) see, is
2 doesn't fit, bring, will (we'll) change
3 Will I get, pay
4 give, will (we'll) let, arrives
5 will it take, order
6 don't see, want, ask

EXERCISE 2

2 If you don't give us longer holidays, we won't come to work!
3 If you shorten our lunch-break, we'll walk out!
4 If you don't improve safety standards, we'll stop work!
5 If you don't provide better working conditions, we won't do overtime!
6 If you don't introduce a shorter working week, we'll complain to the union!

EXERCISE 3

2 unless
3 provided (that)/as long as/so long as
4 in case
5 provided that/as long as/so long as
6 Supposing

EXERCISE 4

(Suggested answers)

1 we lose the way/we get lost
2 you drive carefully/you don't drive too fast
3 it gets lost
4 it's not too expensive/it's in good condition

5 the weather is good/it's warm enough
6 we hurry/we walk faster/we leave now

EXERCISE 5

2 If he went on a diet, he'd lose weight.
3 If he took some exercise, he'd get fit.
4 If he stopped drinking, he'd live longer.
5 If he ate the right food, he'd feel better.
6 If he took care of his health, he'd enjoy life more.

EXERCISE 6

2	would you choose	11	tried	18	wouldn't hurt
3	would (I'd) get	12	would (it'd) fall	19	didn't eat
4	didn't have	13	had	20	Would either of you be
5	would (I'd) take	14	would (I'd) want	21	would (I'd) find
6	would (I'd) be able	15	would you catch	22	didn't speak
7	Would you try	16	didn't have	23	would (I'd) enjoy
8	managed	17	would (there'd) be	24	would (I'd) begin
9	would (I'd) try				
10	wouldn't try				

EXERCISE 7

2 I wouldn't say it unless it were true.
3 Supposing we rented a car, would you be prepared to share the driving?
4 I'll tell you what he said, so long as you promise not to tell anyone.
5 In case you're home before me, I'll give you the spare key.
6 If you paid more attention, you'd know what I was talking about!
7 You can have the room for as long as you like, provided you pay the rent on time!
8 I don't mind you having a party, as long as you don't make too much noise.

EXERCISE 8

2 If I'd seen him, I wouldn't have pulled out.
3 If he'd looked carefully, he would have seen me.
4 If he hadn't pulled out in front of me, I wouldn't have had to brake suddenly.
5 If the Jaguar hadn't been so close behind me, the driver would have been able to stop.
6 If the driver in front hadn't braked suddenly, I wouldn't have hit him.
7 If I hadn't wanted to overtake him, I wouldn't have been so close behind him.
8 If he hadn't been such a slow driver, I wouldn't have wanted to overtake him.

EXERCISE 9

(Suggested answers)

2 If the roof had landed any nearer/had hit us/hadn't missed us, we would/might/could have been killed/injured.
3 If they had listened to the weather reports, they wouldn't have gone out in their yacht/would have stayed at home.
4 If he hadn't been so tired/his reactions had been faster, he wouldn't have lost/he would/could/might have won/wouldn't have been knocked out.

5 If he hadn't forgotten/had remembered to post/had posted my entry form, I would have won £10,000.
6 If he hadn't made that remark/had thought before he spoke, he wouldn't have lost his job.

EXERCISE 10

2 had listened/had been listening, would have heard
3 would have had, hadn't left
4 were, wouldn't keep on
5 hear, think
6 stand, will (you'll) be
7 hold, will (you'll) be
8 would climb, could get
9 sees/saw, will (they'll)/would (they'd) call
10 would make, didn't worry
11 move, will (I'll) be
12 hadn't been/weren't, wouldn't have broken

EXERCISE 11

(Suggested answers)

1 we'll go out/have a picnic
2 I'd tell you
3 if he phones/calls/rings
4 I would have lent it to you/wouldn't have been angry/would have told you
5 she won't pass the exam/she'll fail the exam
6 if he didn't need the money
7 you can get up/go back to work on Monday/we'll have a barbecue on Saturday
8 I would have cooked something special/cancelled my appointment
9 you wouldn't be so tired
10 if he'd been more careful/paid attention/taken more care

17 Indirect (Reported) Speech

EXERCISE 1

1 (that) he's having a wonderful time
2 (He says) (that) the weather's superb.
3 (He says) (that) he's/(he has) been to the Grand Canyon.
4 (He says) (that) he hopes to have a trip to Mexico.
5 (He says) (that) he wishes he could stay longer, but (that) it's too expensive.
6 (He says) (that) he's coming back at the end of the month.

EXERCISE 2

2 (that) they were extremely lucky to have a short working day and long holidays
3 He said (that) the Government was not prepared to pay them more for doing nothing.
4 He said (that) the Teachers' Union had to accept that fact.

5 He said (that) if they went on strike, they would be acting totally irresponsibly.
6 (that) he was extremely angry at the Minister's remarks.
7 He said (that) teachers were hard-working, responsible people.
8 He said (that) when they went home they could not relax because they had to mark books and prepare lessons.
9 He said (that) he had been teaching for twenty years, and during that time the pay and conditions had gone down.
10 He said (that) the Minister had no idea what he was talking about and should resign.

EXERCISE 3

2	apologise	5	advise	8	suggest	11	threaten
3	offer	6	thank	9	promise	12	agree
4	warn	7	announce	10	admit		

(Pronouns are suggestions only.)

2 He apologised for being late.
3 He offered to carry my case/the case for me.
4 He warned her not to touch the switch (because it was dangerous).
5 I advised her to see a doctor (about it).
6 She thanked her for looking after the baby (for her).
7 She announced (that) they had decided to get married.
8 She suggested going/that they should go by train.
9 He promised to pay me back tomorrow/the next day.
10 He admitted breaking the speed limit.
11 She threatened to tell their father (if they didn't stop doing that immediately).
12 She agreed (with me) that it was difficult.

EXERCISE 4

2 you hadn't (did not have) any more in stock then/at that time
3 you were expecting a delivery later on that day
4 they would be there about three o'clock that afternoon
5 (if I liked) he would phone me
6 you would deliver one the next/following day

EXERCISE 5

1 what experience I'd (I had) had
2 she asked me if/whether I could type, write shorthand and use a telex machine
3 she asked me if/whether I had (I'd got) any qualifications
4 she asked me why I'd (I had) left my last job
5 she asked me how long I'd (I had) been looking for another job
6 she asked me if/whether I wanted to work in an office again
7 she asked me if/whether I was looking for a full-time or a part-time job
8 she asked me when I could start work

EXERCISE 6

1 asked her what to say/what he should say at his daughter's wedding
2 asked her who to write to/who she should write to about the postal service
3 asked her what to wear/what she should wear to her husband's office party

4 asked her how to help/how she could help her son learn to read
5 asked her where to go/where he should go for/to get legal advice
6 asked her how to stop/how she could stop her daughter biting her nails

EXERCISE 7

1 to stay/(that) I should/must stay in my room after dinner
2 told me to eat/(that) I should/must eat my meals in the kitchen, not the dining-room
3 She told me not to bring/(that) I shouldn't/couldn't bring my friends to the house.
4 she told me not to use/(that) I shouldn't/couldn't/mustn't use the telephone.
5 she told me to take/(that) I should/must take my shoes off when I come indoors.
6 she told me not to make/(that) I shouldn't/mustn't make a noise after nine o'clock.
7 She told me not to use/(that) I shouldn't/couldn't/mustn't use the bathroom after 8.00 p.m.
8 she told me to smoke/(that) I should/must smoke in the garden, not the house.

EXERCISE 8

2 if/whether there was any more news about the *Columbus*
3 said/replied (that) he had had another telex from the captain the day before/the previous day
4 said (that) the ship was still in Sydney Harbour and could not be unloaded because of the dockers' strike
5 asked if/whether the crew on the *Columbus* could unload the ship themselves
6 said (that) it was out of the question
7 said (that) the union would stop every ship in the company
8 told Mr McManus to let him know/(that) he should let him know as soon as he had any news
9 said (that) he understood there was a problem with the *Magellan*
10 asked Mr Greaves what he knew about it
11 said (that) the *Magellan* had broken down in the Mediterranean two days before
12 said (that) they were going to take the ship into Malta for repairs
13 asked Mr Greaves how long the repairs would take
14 said/replied (that) they shouldn't take longer than two or three days, but (that) they might have to wait for spare parts
15 asked Mr Wates how much the repairs would cost
16 said/replied (that) he had (got) an estimate for $20,000, but (that) that did not include the port charges
17 asked Mr Greaves if/whether he was planning to supervise the repairs himself
18 said (that) he was and (that) his flight to Malta left the next/following morning

18 Prepositions

EXERCISE 1

2 next to the cinema
3 between the supermarket and the cinema
4 on the corner/near the bank
5 opposite the garage/next to the bus-stop
6 outside/next to the library

EXERCISE 2

2 to
3 at/outside/in front of
4 across
5 through
6 over/across
7 up
8 round/around
9 down
10 to/towards
11 along
12 under
13 into
14 at/outside/in front of/by

EXERCISE 3

2 between
3 till/until, on
4 by
5 at
6 in
7 until/till, during
8 from, to/till/until

EXERCISE 4

2 until/till
3 after
4 between
5 during/in
6 in
7 in
8 on
9 from
10 to/till/until
11 before
12 on
13 for
14 by/on
15 within/in
16 since
17 in

EXERCISE 5

1 the parcel with a knife
2 against nuclear weapons
3 finish the race in spite of the pain/being in pain
4 the problem by himself
5 is going down, according to the Government
6 told anyone except Barbara
7 without thinking
8 any (other) foreign language besides French
9 a flat with a friend
10 Alec despite her parents' disapproval
11 accept a cheque without a cheque card
12 everything apart from clean/cleaning the bathroom

EXERCISE 6

1 (b) talks about   (c) getting bored with   (d) thinking of
2 (a) worried about   (b) shouting at   (c) agree on   (d) believe in
3 (a) thinking about   (b) suffer from   (c) ask (her) for   (d) laugh at
4 (a) look at   (b) getting tired of   (c) complain about   (d) agree with

EXERCISE 7

2	next to/beside/in front of	11	at	20	behind
3	about	12	with	21	in front of/near
4	in	13	at	22	against
5	besides/apart from/except	14	without	23	in/into
6	under	15	on	24	until/till/before
7	behind	16	by	25	except/apart from
8	after/before	17	on	26	before
9	during	18	out of/through		
10	on	19	since		

EXERCISE 8

2	at	15	in	28	near
3	by	16	for	29	inside
4	for	17	by	30	until/till
5	at	18	for	31	in spite of/despite
6	until/till	19	below	32	in
7	from	20	with	33	throughout
8	from	21	on	34	during
9	on	22	in	35	by
10	about	23	under/underneath/beneath	36	above
11	between	24	Among/Amongst	37	except/apart from
12	across/over	25	to	38	from
13	during/at	26	from		
14	towards	27	out of		

19 Phrasal Verbs

EXERCISE 1

1	down	3	on with	5	out of	7	off	9	up
2	off	4	down	6	up with	8	down on	10	in

EXERCISE 2

1 get on with his father-in-law
2 look after the baby
3 (a) make up an excuse   (b) make an excuse up
4 run out of petrol
5 (a) fill in this form   (b) fill this form in
6 carry on with the lesson

EXERCISE 3

2	b	3	b	4	a	5	a	6	a	7	b	8	a	9	b	10	b

EXERCISE 4

1	it on	4	him off	7	it back	10	me down
2	forward to it	5	on with it	8	out of it		
3	up with it	6	it out	9	up with it		

EXERCISE 5

(Suggested answers)

2 Yes, I didn't get in till 9.15/I was held up in the traffic.
3 I get on with her all right/We don't get on very well.
4 I'm getting/I've got over it, thanks.
5 Oh, sorry, I meant to give it back/Haven't I given it back to you?
6 No, you'll have to look it up.
7 Yes, I'm looking for a pair of boots/Can I try on this jacket?
8 Why don't you take off your jacket?/Shall I turn off the fire/central heating?

20 Linking Words

EXERCISE 1

2 the beaches are empty and the sea is clear blue
3 It's neither crowded nor commercialized
4 Life is quiet, but there's plenty to do
5 You can either rent an apartment or you can stay in a two-star hotel.
6 The accommodation isn't luxurious, but it's clean and comfortable.
7 either phone 01 762 9292 or call into our offices

EXERCISE 2

(Suggested answers)

2 After returning/When/After/As soon as I returned to England, I applied for a three-year architectural course
3 While/When I was studying at Manchester University, I developed an interest in photography
4 I left the university in April 1980, before taking/I took my final exams in June
5 (I) worked for an advertising agency until I had saved enough money
6 Since qualifying/I qualified, I have been employed by the *Daily News*
7 as soon as/when/after my contract finishes in April, I shall be available to start a new job (immediately)

EXERCISE 3

1 I'll look after the children until you get back.
2 As soon as the programme ends, I'll come to bed.
3 will you ask him to phone me when he comes in
4 Once the plane lands, you'll feel much better.
5 I'll check it before I go out.
6 Shall I wait in the car while you're in the bank?

EXERCISE 4

(Suggested answers)

1 I couldn't phone you last night as/because/since I left your number at work.
2 The flight was delayed because of snow/because there was snow on the runway.
3 The train was cancelled. That's why/That's the reason why I was late.
4 He failed his driving test because/as he didn't stop at the red lights.
5 I'd better meet him at the station as/since/because he doesn't know the way.
6 It was far too expensive. That's why/That's the reason why I didn't buy it.

EXERCISE 5

2 the china and glass were packed so badly/so badly packed that a number of valuable pieces were broken
3 the men refused to carry any heavy furniture upstairs so that I had to carry it myself
4 As a result I injured my back and, consequently, I have had to take a week off work.
5 I should receive some compensation for the damage and inconvenience. Therefore, I have written to my solicitor

EXERCISE 6

2 But
3 On the other hand/However
4 However/On the other hand
5 whereas/while
6 although

EXERCISE 7

(Suggested answers)

1 She had to get a visa to go to/visit America.
2 I'll post her card early so that it arrives/gets there on time.
3 He gave up his career in the navy in order to spend/have more time/be with his family
4 He turned his radio down so as not to wake/disturb his flatmate.
5 They decided to emigrate to Australia in order that their children might have a better future.
6 She joined a club so as to make new friends/meet more people.

EXERCISE 8

2 not as well cooked as
3 as efficient as
4 as friendly as
5 not as relaxed as
6 not as expensive as
7 not as good as

EXERCISE 9

(Suggested answers)

2 as, as
3 whereas/while
4 Consequently/Therefore/As a result
5 that's why/that's the reason why/therefore
6 since/as/because
7 However/On the other hand
8 In order to/So as to/To
9 but/however
10 as soon as/when/once
11 because of
12 since
13 as, as
14 so that/in order that
15 either
16 or
17 as/since/because
18 as soon as/when/once

21 Punctuation

EXERCISE 1

The following words should begin with a capital letter:

1 I'm, Brenda, Victoria Station, Saturday, We'll, Bond Street, Shaftesbury Avenue
2 Sir Richard Algrave, British Ambassador, Brazil, He, South American, Oxford University, Portuguese, He, Christmas
3 What, Scotland, Loch Ness Monster (monster), Well, Grampian Mountains, Isle, Skye, Interested, We're, September, For, Highland Tours, Regent Street, London, W4

EXERCISE 2

1 Unfortunately, Prof. Maurice Spitz is unable to give tonight's lecture. However, we are very pleased to welcome Dr Edmund Johnston instead. Dr Johnston, as many of you will know, is an expert in Middle Eastern affairs.
2 Certain foods, e.g. eggs, milk, cheese, butter, etc., are unhealthy if eaten in large quantities. On the other hand, bread and potatoes, traditionally considered fattening, are very important in a healthy diet.
3   West Worth Co. Ltd
        The company's annual dinner and dance will be held at
the Queen's Hotel, Wallace Rd, Epsom, on Sat. Dec. 5th at 8.00 p.m.

EXERCISE 3

1 "Hands up!" he shouted. "Don't move!"
   "What do you want?" the bank manager asked, knowing very well what the answer would be.
   "What do you think?"/"!" replied the man coldly. "Now give me the keys to the safe!"
2 "Help!"
   "What was that?" asked Toby.
   "I didn't hear anything," his friend Gerry replied.
   "I thought I heard someone call "help!". It sounded like a woman's voice. Listen! There it is again! Come on, let's see what's wrong!"
3 Ray and Eddy watched in astonishment as Paul stopped the Porsche outside Eddy's house.
   "What a fantastic car!" said Ray.
   "Where did you get it?" asked Eddy.
   Paul enjoyed seeing the look of astonishment on his friends' faces.
   "It's my brother's car," he said. "He's lent it to me while he's away."
   "You lucky thing!" said Ray. "Can we have a go?"

EXERCISE 4

(Suggested answer)

Vegetables are for everyone — not just vegetarians! And yet we, the British, eat fewer vegetables annually (eighty-five kilos per person) than most other Europeans. However, this may all change now that more people are becoming interested in growing their own.

Home-grown vegetables have three definite advantages over shop-bought ones: you can choose the kinds of vegetables you wish to grow; you can pick and eat them the moment they are ready; you can save money — not to mention the satisfaction of having grown them yourself!

In this book we have included thirty-five different types of vegetables. Some are old favourites (carrots, lettuces, potatoes) while others are less well known. And, in addition, we have included a special section on growing herbs (pages 116–19).

Which vegetables you choose to grow — the old favourites or something new — is entirely up to you.

EXERCISE 5

1

Dear Bill,
    Congratulations! I hear you've been promoted to managing director. How about meeting for lunch to celebrate? We'll be away for a week in mid-Aug. — the annual visit to my mother-in-law's home in Ireland — but we'll be back on the twenty-fourth. Why don't you give me a ring so we can arrange something?

    Regards,

    Terry

P.S. Don't know if you've got my new number. It's 9631 ext. 41.

2

Residents of Banbury Road, Ipswich, are angry about yesterday's decision by the local council to allow the Sunday market in Banbury Road to continue. The residents have three main complaints: the excessive noise from 7.00 a.m. every Sunday; the increase in traffic, which endangers children's lives (one child was knocked down last month); the amount of litter in the street after the market closes.

Mrs Hilda West, who has lived in the road for more than twenty-five years, said, "I'm furious! It's all right for the councillors. They don't have to live here. This used to be a quiet road before the market arrived."

The residents now plan to write to their local M.P., William Davis. The council refused to comment on its decision.